# RED, WHITE & BLOWN

**Other titles in *The Crikey Read* series:**
*Lies and Falsehoods* – Bernard Keane
*Unvaxxed* – Dyani Lewis
*Leaning Out* – Kristine Ziwica
*The Teal Revolution* – Margot Saville
*Gen F'd?* – Alison Pennington

**The Crikey. Read**

# RED, WHITE & BLOWN

Is the United States of America a cult?

**GUY RUNDLE**

*Hardie Grant*
BOOKS

Published in 2023 by Hardie Grant Books,
an imprint of Hardie Grant Publishing

Hardie Grant Books (Melbourne)
Wurundjeri Country
Building 1, 658 Church Street
Richmond, Victoria 3121

Hardie Grant Books (London)
5th & 6th Floors
52–54 Southwark Street
London SE1 1UN

hardiegrant.com/books

All rights reserved. No part of this publication may be reproduced, stored in a retrieval system or transmitted in any form by any means, electronic, mechanical, photocopying, recording or otherwise, without the prior written permission of the publishers and copyright holders.

The moral rights of the author have been asserted.

Copyright text © Guy Rundle 2023

 A catalogue record for this book is available from the National Library of Australia

Red, White and Blown
ISBN 978 1 74379 958 1

10 9 8 7 6 5 4 3 2 1

Cover design by Josh Durham/Design by Committee
Typeset in Adobe Caslon Pro by Cannon Typesetting

Printed in Australia by Griffin Press, an Accredited ISO AS/NZS 14001 Environmental Management System printer.

 The paper this book is printed on is certified against the Forest Stewardship Council® Standards. Griffin Press holds FSC® chain of custody certification SCS-COC-001185. FSC® promotes environmentally responsible, socially beneficial and economically viable management of the world's forests.

Hardie Grant acknowledges the Traditional Owners of the country on which we work, the Wurundjeri people of the Kulin nation and the Gadigal people of the Eora nation, and recognises their continuing connection to the land, waters and culture. We pay our respects to their Elders past and present.

# CONTENTS

| | |
|---|---:|
| Introduction: January 2023 | 1 |
| **1.** Cult USA | 13 |
| **2.** The US cult of exceptionalism | 28 |
| **3.** Awakening America | 48 |
| **4.** Two Americas, but not the ones you think | 61 |
| **5.** Countercults and the cult of progressivism | 84 |
| **6.** The founding | 109 |
| Conclusion: American reason | 116 |
| Acknowledgements | 130 |
| Notes | 131 |

To Jonathan Green, whose fault this is.

# INTRODUCTION
## JANUARY 2023

Sprawled around the chamber of the US House of Representatives in groups of three and four, or in mini-caucuses of ten or so, the 435 members of the lower chamber of the 118th US Congress talked, argued, joked, ate pizza – and failed to elect a Speaker.

As the world watched through the C-Span livestream of House business, the new Republican-controlled House of Representatives tried and failed fourteen times to elect Kevin McCarthy, the heir presumptive, to the post. The US House Speaker is the leader of the majority party in the House, and thus either an enforcer of the President's legislative agenda, and an agenda of their own, or the de facto leader of the Opposition.

The midterm elections delivered a victory for the Republicans, albeit a narrow one, winning nine seats to come out with 222 in total. The narrow margin left them vulnerable to the actions of any renegade or extreme faction, if there was one. There was one: the Freedom Caucus: twenty or so die-hard 'insurgent' Republicans, who had initially been defined by their slavish devotion to Donald Trump, during his presidency and after. But they had broken away, as Trump threw what remained of his power behind Kevin McCarthy.

Now the Freedom Caucus were operating rogue, and in return for their support they wanted things: seats on key committees, a vote on term limits for congresspeople, and a commitment to refusing to authorise the lifting of the debt ceiling. This last move threatened to create a political crisis and move the US close to debt default if adopted, so the stakes were high.

When the House convened on Tuesday 3 January, few people expected McCarthy to win the vote on the first ballot. Most likely the Freedom Caucus would hold out for a couple minor concessions and a couple of ballots, to make themselves visible. The Republican victory in the midterms had been shockingly narrow, and they had failed to win control of the senate. There was very little wiggle room. The Democrats had been rock solid in their support of Nancy Pelosi as Speaker before the midterms, and she had driven mercilessly and impressively. Surely, the Republicans could not be so self-defeating as to let themselves look like a rabble, a coalition of groups that formed no unified party? Surely they could not let the parliament of the most powerful country in the world drift leaderless?

They could and they did, for fifteen ballots, as the capacity of the most powerful country in the world to govern itself was thrown into question. Finally, with some arguably treasonous congresspeople appointed to national security committees, the speakership was won for Kevin McCarthy. Order was restored. And then unrestored as a threat to refuse to lift the debt ceiling was made. As this book goes to press, Florida governor Ron DeSantis is beginning his presidential run, based on a state regime of emptying schools of all books (in case some are contentious), staging state takeovers of 'woke' public colleges, and making the still-legal 'morning-after' pregnancy termination pill unobtainable in his state – and gaining Republican plaudits for it all. And in early April 2023 a new stage is beginning. Donald Trump has recently been indicted to stand trial on multiple felony counts, for alleged falsification of business records connected to 'hush' money payments to women and former associates. Even now, mainstream Republican leaders refuse to distance themselves from the Donald.

What the hell is going on? Who are these people? What has happened to the US – the Cold War colossus, the sole superpower? Is this politics or is it something else? And how the hell has it come to this? From, of all things, a midterm election?

* * *

From 1990 to 2014, the turnout for midterm elections (congressional elections held in the middle of a president's four-year term) never rose above 41 per cent, and was often in the 30s. A chunk of the population simply assumed that elections were a once every four years occasion, with all the presidential ra-ra, and that congresspeople – when they thought about them at all – had four-year terms (but actually, members of the House of Representatives serve two-year terms, while members of the Senate serve six-year terms).

In the last couple of decades, such ignorance has been enormously helpful to the Republicans, since non-awareness of the midterms was largely focused among younger voters and the less well educated (the so-called 'low information' voter). The GOP ('Grand Old Party', the Republican Party's nickname) relied on this, and could manage to get their older, whiter, angrier voters to the polls, to essentially ambush the youthquake votes occurring at presidential elections, and take control of Congress, state governorships and much else besides. That was what happened to Barack Obama in 2010, when he lost sixty-three House seats and observed that he had got a 'shellacking' (an Australianism he picked up in Indonesia and introduced to American discourse); and again in the presidential election in 2012; and to Bill Clinton in 1994 and 1998. The same hadn't happened to Republicans under Dubya in 2002, and they only lost congressional power narrowly in the 2006 midterm elections, after twelve years in control.

Until recently, midterm elections had such low turnouts that the whole game was just making sure your voters got to the polls in an unglamorous and unfocused election. But since the coming of Trump, that's all changed. In 2018, voter turnout in the 2018 midterm elections hit 48 per cent.[1] This was up from the 2014 midterm turnout of 34 per cent – a near 50 per cent increase in turnout.

So the assumption going into the 2022 midterms was that the Joe Biden administration was about to get whatever was one level above a shellacking.

The Biden administration had, from day one of coming to power, been trapped in the jaws of death that was familiar to Democrat administrations. Democrat presidents are elected overwhelmingly by the hard work and campaigning of an army of people that Americans call 'the left' – and who Australians would call the 'very mildly centre-left'. Yet Biden was voted into power by a crucial swing of what Americans would call 'independents' – and we would call the 'mainstream centre-right' – who were voting to keep the Republicans out. From day one, any Democrat administration is engaged in the business of simultaneously disappointing and angering its left base with broken promises, while enraging its independent voters with the few centre-left initiatives it does progress. So it had proved for Joe Biden, a seventy-eight-year-old man, once the epitome of vigour, upon whom the years were finally taking a toll.

Following the 2022 midterm elections and in the wake of two years of COVID, the Biden administration had committed to a large stimulus package of infrastructure building to spend close to $600 billion over ten years, which would not only fill the demand gap in the economy but also allow for the steady replacement of the country's worn-down infrastructure. However, in the lead-up to the 2020 election, the left won a commitment to a massive 'social infrastructure' program attached to the infrastructure program. They weren't going to accept the usual emergency capitalist pump-priming, in which workers got the same shitty wages and conditions, in exchange for having a job. This time workers were going to get subsidised childcare, sick leave, training allowances and much more. Biden was not disinclined to provide such, being a man of the centre-left, and having moved somewhat leftwards in the last ten years.

For the Republicans, this was something to be fought tooth and nail. They wanted the government to start paying down the country's $30 trillion debt – the one they had largely run up themselves – while cutting taxes, reducing services and providing a much smaller stimulus package of around $500 billion.

Problem was, it wasn't just the Republicans who were saying this. Two Democratic senators wanted this too: Joe Manchin, the unlikely Democrat from heavily Republican West Virginia, who had an excuse; and the whacky ex-Green Party radical Krysten Sinema from newly Democrat Arizona, who didn't.[2]

By the time they agreed to pass something, it was also far too late to even begin making a difference to the economic landscape. As the name suggests, the *Inflation Reduction Act* was designed to combat inflation by getting production roaring, and thus draw up some of the excess money sloshing around the society, while also curbing excess corporate profits through increased competition. But, signed into law less than three months before the midterms, it could do nothing. It left the Democrats open to the charge that they didn't care about the most basic life issues, and with the lamest of defences: that this bill would, in a couple of years, deliver some really big things, you just wait ...

As far as 'basic' life issues went, there was dissent in the Democratic camp as to what exactly that meant. In 2020, the Trump administration and the Republicans had achieved their aim of gaining a solid 'conservative' majority on the Supreme Court, with the death of Ruth Bader Ginsburg and the subsequent nomination and confirmation of Amy Coney Barrett. In 2022, the Supreme Court delivered what the right had sought for half a century: the countermanding of the *Roe v Wade* ruling. The 1973 ruling had guaranteed a right to abortion by arguing that there was an implicit right to bodily privacy in the Constitution. The new ruling was in relation to a state's attempts to limit abortion legality to a certain number of weeks post conception, and with tight conditions, and the challenge by a pro-choice organisation against it. In the case of *Dobbs v Planned Parenthood* – Dobbs being the State Health Officer of Mississippi – the Court ruled 6–3 that there was no national right to privacy such as would subtend the right to abortion. There was no ban on abortion; it was a matter for states. Around twenty-five states either immediately created such bans or anti-abortion laws that were created earlier swung into effect.

For millions of progressives, especially younger people, abortion access – now difficult or impossible for more than sixty or so million women and girls – was as 'basic' a life issue there could be.

There was another 'basic' life issue that was also non-economic (although abortion availability is a pretty imperative economic issue), and that was the question of the survival of democracy in these not very United States.

While the midterms were getting underway with a series of primary battles in both parties, the inflation rate bucked and swelled, eating at people's pay packets; and the shell-shocked healthcare sector tried to assemble a pregnancy termination system from ruin, the congressional inquiry into the 6 January 2021 'putsch' against Congress was putting that question front and centre for millions of people.

Memories of the event had died away a little during 2021, after the shock of its occurrence had dissipated, and the relief that it had not succeeded in its aims. But two things happened to bring it back into the public consciousness.

First, the Congressional hearings pulled it apart moment by moment, as the FBI tracked down and charged hundreds of participants. Secondly, there were dozens, perhaps hundreds, of Republicans running for nomination in the primaries, who affirmed that the 2020 election had been stolen, that Donald Trump was the legitimate president, and that the storming of Congress had been just and in defence of the republic.

Midst the widespread disappointment with the Biden administration, the right's unrepentant assertion that they were in the right appeared to be giving them an energy and drive that the divided left lacked. This was despite the fact that the inquiry into 6 January 2021 was revealing a degree of pre-planning, sinister anti-democratic intent and presidential support for a violent coup d'état. With increasing alarm, mainstream Democrats urged that the 2022 midterm election campaign be focused on democracy and its fragility and protection.

For others in the party however, this was a strategy that would be at best a distraction, and at worst actively counter-productive. Millions of Americans were hugely worried about putting gas in their car (the price of a gallon was now $3.41, where it had been $2.17) and food on their table, as inflation bit and wages took the hit. They didn't feel they lived in a particularly democratic society, having little power over the course of their daily lives, lives that had suddenly become very difficult in the past twelve months. To many, the 6 January putsch had been a bunch of crazies going too far. There may have been mayhem, and the deaths of police officers and so on. But the worst hadn't happened, and the rather confronting stories about the mob banging on the door of various politicians' offices did not really enter the public's consciousness.

INTRODUCTION

There was so much dislike of politicians anyway, that many people found it hard to find sympathy.

Through the middle of 2022 then, there was a tussle within the centre of the Democratic Party as to what weight would be put on these issues. When key operatives looked at the possibilities and the polls, many said they felt vaguely nauseous. Bread-and-butter economic issues were uppermost, but there was no immediate record to defend. Abortion and other such issues were moving the youth to frenzied engagement, but might be actively turning away voters who were socially conservative working class types. The call to defend democracy and the republic, pitched as an appeal to the nobility of the American people and project, might come off as pompous and unreal. After all, seventy-one million people had voted for Donald Trump in 2020, knowing exactly what he was. If they were willing to tolerate all that – voters the Democrats needed to persuade back – why would they care about a small skirmish around and inside the Capitol building? In the lead up to the campaign, there was furious debate at the highest levels of the Democratic leadership as to whether these issues of social policy and governance were the ticket to victory in a changing society, or the ultimate folly – a disaster fomented by a self-regarding new class of progressives, out of touch with the mass of American people, but now in control of the party apparatus itself.

### A republic, if they can keep it

Well, you know the result – the details and implications of which I'll explore in this book. This short examination of that period is about exploring the cracks and contradictions in the

American project that were made visible by this testing election. Some of these fissures and bucklings are recent, some are the product of decades, and some of the root cracks can be seen in the founding of the republic itself.

The question that has been asked repeatedly since the election of Donald Trump, and then his attempted coup, and most urgently at these midterms was: can the republic survive? Oft quoted was Benjamin Franklin's remark, as he came out of the 1787 Constitutional Convention, to a woman who asked him: 'Mr Franklin, what have you given us?' Franklin's reply: 'A republic, if you can keep it.'

Since the end of the Civil War in 1865, there has never been any doubt that the republic could be held together. By the end of World War I, it had become the anchor of a global system of expanding capitalism and nationhood, even if, until World War II, it purported to stay within its borders. After World War II, it was the unashamed global superpower, guaranteeing and dominating most of the world. In 2003, its invasion of Iraq had still been performed in the 'stoop to conquer' mode, a late entrant in the pseudo-wars such as the invasions of Grenada, Panama and the first Gulf War of 1990 by which it policed its world. Thus, too, the Iraq invasion. But not the occupation.

The question of whether the republic would hold together moved from the margins into the centre with Barack Obama, right-wing dissidents wondered how they could leave a country which appeared to have enthroned progressivism, and whose sense of continuity they preserved through psychic defence of 'birtherism' – the belief that Barack Obama was a Kenyan ring-in by the 'new world order'. If anything, it was the re-election of Obama, rather than his 2008 elevation, that legitimised this notion of a broken republic. Once could be put down to fluke and aberration; twice was a statement of intent by the American people, or a majority of them anyway. Then came Trump.

And the Republican response to the perceived failures of the Biden administration? Not to promote the return of a rational centre-right program that spoke to the country of hard choices and offered them a planned way out. No, it was simply another blizzard of ludicrous paranoia suggesting that the Biden administration was un-American, actively controlled by foreign agents and sinister global forces, and that Biden's son Hunter and various dodgy dealings in the Ukraine were tied up in this.

The movement was starting to give the appearance of a cult: a movement built around a series of simple prophetic truths tied to great figures, and capable of transforming and reproducing itself while keeping true to its faith. There had been a lot of loose talk about the Trump cult, but now it was continuing after the founding figure himself was out of the action, and already much diminished. Was the cult a lot wider than the Trump era?

Could it be that the whole country is a cult?

The suggestion that the US is a cult with a nation attached is not intended metaphorically, but literally. I am suggesting that it is a different type of entity, that it is not steered by the same mix of tradition, ethnos, make-do and layered self-definition by which other nations define themselves. In exploring this theme in such a short volume, vast amounts of the country's history and politics can only be referred to in passing, or omitted altogether. This is emphatically not presented as 'The Shortest Possible History of the United

States', and some currents have gained little mention – the current evangelical movement, for example – because they are exhaustively covered elsewhere. The intellectual history behind this 'cult-based' approach has been consigned to the endnotes. But the notion of the US as a 'cult' is not an arbitrary framing. By thinking of the country in these terms, the nation's history, difference, current conditions and, most importantly, future actions become far more comprehensible than they would otherwise be.

The notion that the US is a cult – founded before its revolution, producing that as an event, and then forming itself and world history through fidelity to that cult – reshapes not only our thoughts of what one expects the US to do, but of our relationship to it. That's especially true for Australians, but really a matter of import for anyone in the West, in an era when the great nations' sense of themselves – in China, in India, in the US – may determine the future of our planet.

# 1.
# CULT USA

With all this malarkey coming from the Republicans, the midterms thus threatened to be the return of the type of politics that had elected Trump: mythical, identifying system and law itself as enemies of freedom, paranoid in style, and steered by the polestar belief that there was a simple solution to all the woes of society and personal life, which, when discovered, would bring on a golden age.

This had been the inspiration for the Trump base in 2015 and 2016. They comprised about 25 per cent of registered Republicans, which means they made up about 7.5 per cent of the population[3] – the sort of fringe-core element one might find in any modern society. But the system of primary elections for party candidates, and the vast field of candidates opposing Trump, had allowed the chaotic Trump circus to turn the Republican Party as a whole into their megaphone, and then attract a crucial majority of voters in the right states to win power.

Of course, most people who voted for Trump in 2016 had not signed on to the whole Trump-cult package: the wide-eyed belief that this bogus billionaire was some sort of earthly god who could restore the nation's lost greatness through his sheer personality. Most were hardcore Republicans who would have voted for a cactus over any Democratic candidate. The rest were voters taken from the Democrats in rust belt states like Pennsylvania and Michigan, who either had an informed opinion that Trump's idea of tariffs and a trade war with China would return 'good jobs' to the US, or tended to express the thought that Trump 'was a businessman, not a politician' and might be able to cut through the stagnation and corruption of Washington.

But the crucial questions I pondered while travelling the US in the *annus amazingus* of 2016 were: how many Trump voters were rational and strategic actors? And how many were drawn in by the glow of the Trump phenomenon and the teasing paradox of a man descending in a gold elevator in a black skyscraper named after him, presenting himself as the champion of the people? These were questions I could never answer fully to my satisfaction while vox popping at rallies, bars and in Midwest diners. No sooner had I spoken to one ex-auto worker, a union man or woman, about NAFTA and the closing of the profitable factory they worked in, the lack of any replacement jobs, and how this disqualified Hillary Clinton from getting their vote, than the person on the next stool down the counter would turn around and tell me about how the Clintons had had all the gold in Fort Knox replaced with painted bricks on the orders of George Soros to create a world currency. Sometimes, these tendencies were present in the same person, with a discussion of the need for a genuine public insurance option in the health system segueing into a rave about Obama's retrofitted Hawaiian childhood.

There had been nothing of this scale and volatility in the 2012 election, with the right having no one to rally around except the hapless Mitt Romney – a man whose politics were extreme right on the Australian scale, but moderate centre-right in the US context.

True, the election of Obama, and the very limited bail-out of mortgage-holders had generated the 'Tea Party' – an insurgent group within and without the Republican Party that was partly a genuine grassroots movement, partly a creature of Fox News. The Tea Party was a 'fidelist' movement, a movement of faith to the revolution.[4] Everything had gone wrong in the US, they said, because the country had drifted from the Constitution that was created at its founding. Tea Partiers began holding rallies in eighteenth-century garb – with frock coats, muskets and tricorne hats; usually in Walmart carparks – grooving on the incongruity of it all. Their most radical supporters had an anarchist or 'minarchist' (absolutely minimum government) vibe, suggesting that nothing other than the Constitution was required to govern the US, and that Congress should therefore vote itself out of existence. The other element was Ayn Randism, an absolute obsession. The Tea Partiers loved Rand's sense of the dynamic, promethean individual who was nevertheless put upon and repressed by the sinister forces of collectivism. 'Who is John Galt?', they graffitied at rallies, in homage to the hero of Rand's *Atlas Shrugged*.

The Tea Partiers had a dose of conspiracy thinking about them, but they were still a recognisable political movement, with clear ideas of rational political action. They were a cheery bunch, positive about the possibility of 'taking their country back' through democratic means. I did enjoy some of their rallies, especially the travelling roadshow with the Sarah Palin impersonator.

Trump's triumph in the 2016 election had immediately created a problem for the new president and his followers. He now had to deliver. Within four years he needed to 'make America great again', and in the way that he had described it to his followers. The factories needed to come back to the heartland; there would need to be good jobs a-plenty.

### The 'good jobs' Mirage-a-Lago

'Good jobs': That mantra of the Trumpians, by which was meant: well-paid jobs requiring no special skills, jobs that you could walk into straight out of school where you never got your diploma, or much of an education at all. From World War II until the 1980s, many millions of Americans bought a house and put their kids through college on a single wage from one of those good jobs. Though the post-war period was an exception rather than the rule in the history of industrial capitalism, it coincided with the US's rise to global dominance as the supreme superpower, and the baby boom which greatly increased the population. A massive culture industry of movies, music and TV provided the backdrop for the imagination of possibility and the good life. So, for two generations growing up within this period, it was simply the norm, against which any historical shift would be seen not as political and social change, but as a deviation from the way things should be.

This was what Trump's supporters wanted most of all. The 'greatness' was not the world military domination of the Reagan years. Nor was it the greatness of the American constitutional spirit, of the fight against tyranny. The greatness was in the individual life, in not simply scratching to reproduce yourself body and soul, from one paycheck to the next, which had become the new American norm. 'Every man a king', the Louisiana populist politician Huey Long had said in 1934. The promise of America was to be a king in your own house, with your own big car, your own recliner armchair before the big-screen TV, in a job with a (relatively) high hourly wage, medical and dental insurance, and a retirement fund. That was America. That was what would be great again.

The key problem with this plan was that Trump had no driving urge to make it happen, and lacked the diligence to do so even if he had had one. Also the vast state investment required to make it happen would never have been permitted by the Republicans anyway. The world of high-employment factories in the West could never be restored.

Throughout the 2016 presidential campaign, Trump advocated imposing tariffs to prevent cheap imports from undermining domestic production. The notion that the single measure of tariffs, especially against China, could restore American prosperity dovetailed well with a paranoid notion that the country's difficulties were caused by an external enemy – and coincided neatly with racist notions of sinister and inscrutable 'Orientals' undermining a 'White' nation. But tariffs imposed without directed investment and a plan for reconstruction would do nothing.

And that is exactly what happened. The tariff walls Trump imposed in 2018 did not significantly slow the closure and transfer of factories to the global South, especially Mexico. And factories with export markets suffered greatly as the EU and China responded in kind to Trump's protectionist policies.

## Across the new great divide

By around 2018–19, people in the Midwest were starting to get the picture that nothing was going to change.

The new 'great divide' had opened up in American society in the years immediately before the Trump era. This gulf of opportunity, possibility and wealth arose between those who had a college education (and a goodish one at that), and those who did not. The cause was the deep structural shift in the US, from an industrial society based around manual labour and routine office work, to a knowledge/information one, in which technical and scientific work, cultural production and more complex administrative work became dominant.

This new form of labour required a new social class and, from the 1980s, the US and other Western countries had been expanding higher education. By the 2010s, more than 35 per cent of Americans had a college degree.[5] From the 1990s, Silicon Valley and the tech revolution took off, and so too did culture industries, in response to consumption demand from a wealthier populace.

This new 'knowledge class' became more than a mere subgroup. They numbered many millions, formed a big-spending audience and a powerful political bloc, and they were starting to transform cities, moving into old working-class inner-city areas and reshaping them to their preferences.

They were not simply a branch of the middle class. They had their own distinctive culture and psychology, which was one of cosmopolitanism, universalism and an insistence on the project of social equality as it applied to questions of gender, race, sexuality, gender identity, disability and other social divisions. This came from both the actual content of college courses, as taught by a leftish academy, but also from the form of critical thinking and innovative acting that such education imparted and their work shaped. Why is the US the best country in the world? Why should it run the world? Such questions have been big around campuses and the 'new left' since the 1960s. But now it became the way of approaching the world, by a whole class. The result has been the thundering series of culture wars that we continue to live through.

What had been acceptable – the continued dominance of white tastes, white faces, white assumptions in every field, the very slow shift of gender ratios in executive life and so on – was now depicted as utterly intolerable in the present, and inexcusable in the past. Since the deep principle of modernity was a notion of universal equality, much of this was impossible to argue with. But it was a culture that was owned by the knowledge class, an expression of their power over social life. The archetypal villain of their rhetoric was the rich old white man of the ruling class. But the class that was most affected by this shift in social culture and economic conditions was the industrial working class.

From the 1970s, the US working class was battered by years of stagflation and the vast unemployment and division of the Reagan era. The rewards of the 80s and 90s boom favoured one higher section of the class, as a minority sank into permanent poverty – without having the numbers to take electoral action against a more prosperous majority. In the 2000s and 2010s, the global economy came for the 'upper working class', with offshoring, the 2008 crash, thousands of factories heading south and east, and whole states reduced to the status of 'rust belt'.

The working class had lost their economic heft, and their culture – the post-war heritage of Elvis, Brando, Monroe and Jimi; of big cars and muscle bikes, military service and the flag; of feeling good to be an American – was coming under attack as well. Called out as sexist, racist and homophobic, millions felt like they were being extinguished from American life and history.

They also felt unrepresented. Mitt Romney didn't do it for them and neither did Ted Cruz. Donald Trump did. He was taking on the people who were telling you how to talk and what to think, and that what you had thought was wrong. He would also bring the 'good jobs' back, and with them the lost world of working-class life would be restored.

This massive and unforgiving transformation had already started to spread conspiracy thinking beyond the usual small corners of esoteric paranoia. The United States' long history of conspiratorial thinking had been hugely revived in the wake of the 9/11 attacks, from rational doubt about the official version of a plan missed by state bungling – sceptics asked if spy agencies had let the attack go through, as a 'fundraiser' – to the idea that the destruction had been a controlled demolition, and eventually, that the planes that hit the towers were holograms wrapped around missiles. Through the 2000s, a few left elements and a larger right contingent had signed up to these theories. This was easily rolled over into Obama 'birth trutherism', and then to theories that mass shootings were staged events featuring 'crisis actors'. By the time Trump came along, this trend was well advanced.

Trump's campaign itself was, at the start, not noticeably conspiratorial in its argument. It preferred to present the Democrats as incompetent, typical politicians and liberals, hopeless wimps who had been cheated and outclassed by the Russians and the Chinese. Trump was a businessman,[6] and the type of businessman his audience recognised: not some pencil-necked geek like Mark Zuckerberg, but a big, loud man who built real things, like buildings. That this heroic, triumphant movement would quickly fall into conspiratorialism and cultishness when it could not deliver showed what a substantial presence these things had in American politics and society, and what a driver they were in social action and belief, far greater than in any other Western society.

**The sturm is coming**

The QAnon cult was a doozy, bursting onto the American stage like nothing had for quite some decades.[7] The bizarre phenomenon began in October 2017 as a series of claimed 'drops' of information on the discussion/troll internet site 4chan by a government official signing themselves 'Q'. It then entered the 'meatspace' (real world), as thousands and then hundreds of thousands of Trump supporters began taking up its main themes. Through their hundreds of drops, 'Q' suggested that Donald Trump was at war against the inherited 'deep state' and the 'swamp' – the Washington power establishment that blocked any real change. The deep state and the swamp had been characters in the Trump fantasia during the 2016 election, but now they were given a few twists.

Trump was now collaborating with other parts of the state in his war with them. The aim? To use the good parts of the military, police and so on, to entrap and expose thousands of politicians and civil servants, and have them hauled off to prison for their part in a vast conspiracy. What was that conspiracy? A massive child slavery, prostitution and exploitation ring run by an absolute A-list of figures, from Hillary and Bill Clinton on down.

Conspiracy theories tend to become more concrete and specific as they grow, never resolving to any general principle or abstract theorem. The Q conspiracy folded over itself and surged and doubled, with the notion that the 'persecution' of Donald Trump by the establishment was half-true, but also concealed a trick. Trump and the decent parts of the establishment were creating a charade of persecution to hide Trump's patient, careful and cunning entrapment of this vast web of criminals. Eventually, the Q mythology insisted, but only when the time was right, 'the storm' would come: Trump would launch the final phase of the operation.

The movement had had a prelude, in the circulation of the 'Pizzagate' conspiracy in 2016; an elaborate story of a Hillary Clinton–headed paedophile ring operating from the basement of Comet Ping Pong, a pizza joint in Georgetown, Washington DC, known for being popular with congressional aides and staffers. The name of the joint was enough for it to be subjected to various gnostic transformations and to suggest that it might be a major portal in the global child-sex trafficking operation. In December 2016, a North Carolina man decided to find out, barging into Comet with a rifle, trying to blast open a locked storage cupboard to find the trafficked children. It's a measure of the country's appetite for conspiracy that this mad denouement did not end the absurdity, but propelled it to the greater heights of the full Q cult.

The Q mythology made sense of the world for thousands of people who felt that their lives were being taken from them by mysterious elite forces they did not know or control, but that they now had a champion in the White House they could rally behind. The photos of Trump used by Q devotees were typically those of him giving a sideways smirk as he boarded a plane or 'the beast', the armoured presidential vehicle. Trump's usual face was the rictus of mild unhappiness he carried everywhere with him, as a prisoner of the presidency; the smirk was an occasional twitch captured by high-speed lenses. But in the context of Q blather, it became something else, a knowing sign to his followers that the plan was underway. 'Trust in the plan', Q-sters would remind each other whenever there was a fresh disaster. The more chaotic and futile the Trump presidency became, the more his followers took this to be an ever more masterful dissembling.

Q was probably an elaborate hoax perpetrated by those closely associated with the management of 4chan, and then its successor 8chan – troll channels that had evolved from a Japanese anime fansite.[8] But Q's many followers tended to be people who knew nothing about computers except how to surf the web. The secret knowledge they had was not the abstract knowledge of the elite but the concrete knowledge of the Q myth.

The notion that Trump was part of a grand scheme to do good and save the republic could survive years of his manifest indolence, incompetence and venality. It could even survive Trump's shocking loss of the 2020 election. Trump's push to frame the election as stolen became the final part of 'the plan'. Trump had deepfaked an election loss, and the election fraud would serve to convict the conspirators still further.

Once they were nabbed, Trump would be reinstalled as president. This was first mooted as occurring on 6 January 2021, with the ratification of states' votes by Congress. When that did not occur – despite an insurrection which stormed the building – various other dates were suggested. None of them had any basis in reality, as there is no capacity to 'disqualify' a sitting president and install his rival as the true winner.

For a few months in early 2020, the power of the Q movement was at its height, the impossibility of a way forward making it – in some sort of cockamamy dialectical thinking – all the more certain that the satanic paedophiles would be brought to justice. But soon, for a wider group of Q enthusiasts – the hinterland that its core relied on to reach and convert the masses – the game was pretty much up. From about April 2020 onwards, there was evidence of a mass disenchantment on the chatboards that formed the basis of the Qmmunity's communication. This increased dramatically after Trump lost the election, and, as weeks went by, the result was not reversed. 'Well, what was that all about?' was the tenor of remarks, along with some recognition that they might, just might, have been conned.

### Laptopgate? Really?

After a few months in power, the Biden administration was struggling to get a big bill passed to alleviate the corrosive effect of inflation and get the economy started again. It looked like Democrat incompetence, à la Carter and Clinton – a simple inability to lead.

But as the Biden administration began to falter, the Republicans and the right did not offer a rational alternative plan or even an account of Biden's failings in normal political-economic terms. Instead, they returned to conspiracy theories, in the form of the Hunter Biden laptop scandal.

In the 2010s, Hunter Biden, Joe Biden's 'failson', had, after multiple fallings short, established a shady business career in Ukraine, making deals almost wholly on the strength of his father's name. Joe Biden was accused of being directly involved in those dealings, and of taking payments from them. President Trump's attempt to get evidence of such activities, which he could use in the election, appeared to extend to him making continued military support to Ukraine conditional on the Ukrainian government committing to investigate the matter. In that respect it became a reverse scandal, Russiagate, which targeted Trump. Then, in 2020, following Biden's election, a bizarre twist: it was claimed that a laptop belonging to Hunter Biden had turned up in a repair shop in Delaware, and had been obtained by Trump ally Rudy Giuliani. And it went on from there.

What impressed in 'Laptopgate' was not that the Republicans went hell-for-leather with the scandal. What party wouldn't? It was that they and the wider American right appeared to be placing all their hopes on Laptopgate, not merely as a political feint, but as a story that would explain that the Biden administration was – what? The accusations being made were more than about corruption or rottenness, or even that old notion of un-Americanness. They were accusations that there was some sort of quasi-satanic cabal at the heart of the presidency. Partly out of desperation but mostly out of habit, they were agglutinating more conspiracy to the scandal, until it had sprung to life and become, like Q, a many-headed beast, rampaging across the political landscape.

As the midterms came into view, Trump reappeared, making gnomic statements from his Mar-a-Lago hideyhole, holding the occasional rally. And Republicans were quick to pay obeisance.

But there were new figures, such as Ron DeSantis, the Republican governor of Florida, who had waged war against the pro-trans and 'gender affirmative' movement, and was gaining great traction from the craze sweeping America to remove certain books from libraries. Members of a group called 'Moms For Liberty' had started getting elected to school boards and instructing school libraries to remove certain books, usually of a pro-queer character. The list of books grew quickly to take in many titles that simply dealt with sexual and identity complexity, and which also, in pursuit of eliminating an alleged ideology of 'critical race theory' being smuggled into schools, included books discussing the history of slavery in the US or the life of Martin Luther King.

Decades ago, the political scientist Richard Hofstadter identified 'the paranoid style in American politics' – a certain tendency for movements to foreclose against rational acknowledgement of the opponent's claims to legitimacy through the obsessive imagining of conspiracy.[9] Now here it was again in the twenty-first century. Furthermore, in one of the country's two major parties, the paranoid fringe had now become the centre. Was a state of conspiracy and cult, which never resolved to the rational debates over rights and resources usually seen as the real business of contesting for government, now a permanent feature of US politics? In their obsessive reaching back to the country's glorious founding, had the right 'done a Cloverfield' – waking an annihilating monster they now could not control?

From within his presidency, Trump had reached into the present and the future with his Supreme Court picks – which was exactly why so many evangelical groups had supported him. Barring extraordinary events, he had determined that one branch of government would be conservative, possibly for decades to come. But it was only possible because the court itself, clothed in the robes of rationality, also gave the appearance of being a seance, communing with the dead spirits of the founders to divine their thoughts on assault rifles, Plan B and gay marriage. If the US is a cult, has it been one from its creation?

# 2.
# THE US CULT OF EXCEPTIONALISM

'Cult' is thrown around very easily, often as little more than a label for a group that the speaker doesn't happen to like. But cults do exist of course, and they became particularly visible in the West at the end of the 1960s, as the explosive energy of that decade's social revolutions began to cool and congeal.[10] As the freewheeling yogis and maharishis of the 60s yielded to the austere discipline of the Hare Krishna, as California was consumed by EST and Synanon, as the Godspell wore off and the besuited Moonies appeared, selling flowers at airports or marrying en masse in stadiums, the 70s saw the counter-culture's apocalyptic end and the triumphant rise of Ronald Reagan, who drew the energy of the cult back into politics.

It is easy to see, in retrospect, that the pullulation of such weirdness in the US was in part a response to the global structural shocks being visited on the republic. The Keynesian period of US-led Western growth had shuddered to a halt in the early 1970s and then turned into sharp recession in

1973 as OPEC quadrupled the price of crude oil. The Third World was still in revolt, most of Asia was red and in 1975, two years after US withdrawal, communist North Vietnam was victorious in a war that the US could not win, and which had drained the country of blood and treasure. The years after were dominated by 'stagflation' – simultaneous unemployment and inflation – within which began the deindustrialisation (through globalisation) of what would become known as the Rust Belt. Now, with the American adventure running into the buffers, and in the White House, Jimmy Carter – an austere president who spoke of selflessness and ecology – the era of the cult was really a final reaction to the disappearance of ecstatic promise. Was that era of promise always going to collapse in on itself?

The exuberance, a renewed exuberance, was what one recognised in the Trump movement, and all the more in the Q movement, a third of a century after the great era of the American cult had ended. Politics as cult and conspiracy theory, the paranoid style, was reasserting itself, in a way that could be simply stated: the cult (and conspiracy) is an inextinguishable part of contemporary American political life.

### Politics and cults

More than in any other Western polity, politics in the US can be seen as a battle between the cult and the rational, a battle that takes place within both sides of politics, and in the great left–right political contest of the nation. No sooner is one manifestation of it exploded and discredited than another will rear up. Who will adopt it is not random, but it is not confined to the powerless and the poor. Other countries in the West have had a dose of this, they have been dominated by it in the past and they are getting more of it again, but nothing like the American situation.

The cult combines concrete mythologising, the promise of a simple solution, the action of real enemies as the explanation for loss and defeat, the return of a golden age that corresponds to the cultists' childhood, or a transcending journey to a future otherworld, or both, and a collective endeavour that allows for ongoing face-to-face connection, real friendship and a resistance to the anomie and isolation that is a condition of modern life for many. In the case of the US, this is occurring in a power that is declining – relative to its previous total domination and expanding prosperity – and with no easy prospect of reversing that process. Cults thus arise and grow repeatedly.

Yet that alone cannot explain their wild success in those United States. Other countries have faced the retreat from glory in the decades after World War II, and they produced nothing like the American manic mass drive to avoid rational thinking about reality. If the US is a cult,[11] if its origins are as a cult, it is one that sits within a wider global and historical process, one in which processes so all-encompassing – like modernity itself – have cult origins that are obscured to us by their now universal character in the texture of our lives. In that respect, the US is exceptional in being the carrier of such a cultish modernity founded on a belief in unending human self-transcendence, with all its Promethean capabilities. And destructive ones too. World-annihilatory. Which makes the American cult of interest far beyond the shores of its shining seas.

Americans acknowledge this cult status, but they do not seem to fully recognise it in themselves.[12] America is 'unique', Americans say; it is the exceptional nation, the guardian of humanity's safety, the 'last, best hope of Earth'.[13] This exceptionalism was once held to be necessarily given by God. It is still held that way by millions, but there are millions more who believe some sort of secular version of it, some vague feeling that the principles it expresses are the true and only form of human good. The jingoism of other nations was seen as irrational – Great Russia, etc. – but the US derived the notion of its unique character from the Enlightenment, and from the valuation of reason that was the Enlightenment's essence.

Exceptionalism was at its least explicit in the post-war period – not coincidentally the only genuinely exceptional period, when the US alone could have ended all life on the planet – and returned in force in 1980 when Ronald Reagan triumphantly supplanted Jimmy Carter's complex but somewhat diffident vision with the slogan 'Let's make America great again'. From then on, no presidential candidate could avoid talking about the uniqueness of the US, in either a right-conservative-religious or left-secular-humanist form, if they wanted to have a chance at political success.

Barack Obama – the half-Kansan, half-Kenyan, raised by a Muslim stepfather in Indonesia and then by white grandparents in the colonised island of Hawaii – could not quite bring himself to say the mantra and, in a 2009 interview with the *Financial Times*, tried to come up with a postmodern version of it:

> I believe in American exceptionalism, just as I suspect that the Brits believe in British exceptionalism and the Greeks believe in Greek exceptionalism. I'm enormously proud of my country and its role and history in the world.[14]

This was gobbledygook in the best Obama style, and a measure of how great his leadership was that he got away with it. By 2014, with the midterms looming, a wiser, sadder, more battered Barack Obama said, at a US Military Academy commencement ceremony:

> I believe in American exceptionalism with every fiber of my being. But what makes us exceptional is not our ability to flout international norms and the rule of law; it is our willingness to affirm them through our actions.[15]

To, inevitably, cite *The Simpsons*, 'Say the line, Bart! Yayyyyyy!' No one has tried to buck the system since.

### Lit up on the hill

US exceptionalism began as an explicitly religious notion. The early revolutionaries in Boston, all descendants of the Puritan tradition, were no fatalists; they were men and women of action. But they were also looking for signs that what they were doing was right, and the revolution's early success was taken as a sign of providence, that God wanted this to happen, to restore the rights of man. Even the founding fathers and mothers who weren't Christians were deists who believed in a 'prime mover' whose energies were not random, but pointed in a certain direction.

This religious conception of an exceptional role powered the Americans to create their own country against the might of the British Empire, and then to roll West and dispossess the native Americans, purchase the South and enslave the Caribbean.[16] Once the Civil War was concluded, and the interior frontier between the Mississippi and California was conquered, the US turned its attention elsewhere, going to war to turf the Spanish out of Cuba and then turning westward, annexing the independent state of Hawaii and taking and occupying the Spanish-held Philippines. The US claimed that it was ridding the world of Spain's backward colonialism, but as Mark Twain and others noted, it wasn't exactly handing back the colonies to the colonised. The Filipinos launched a decade-long insurgency against the US occupiers, who responded with great brutality. By 1914, more than a million Filipinos had died resisting US occupation. This did not deter the US from its mission; quite the contrary. It was because the US was the least, best hope of man that practically any amount of depredation was acceptable for the eventual good of the colonised and the world.

Of course, this was the public ideology.[17] By the time the US began its acquisition of an empire it had become a colossus, dominated by huge corporations, and it required both plentiful raw materials and new markets. From the 1870s, the European powers had carved up the world with new colonies; from 1900, the US was getting what both ideological and business leaders believed to be its share. From the Philippines occupation on, a pattern was set; the US would use its now substantial navy, marines and army to subdue any nations it found recalcitrant. This was applied particularly to the Caribbean and Central America, something that continued as an exception in the 'isolationist period' of 1921–39 when it attempted to withdraw from global engagements, while still maintaining Hawaii and other Pacific islands and control of Central America as allegedly forward defence.

But with Franklin D Roosevelt's reorientation of the country to global involvement, a liberal, world-expansive notion of US exceptionalism came roaring back. Now it had unquestioned power on its side. By the end of World War II (a conflict that had begun with cavalry charges), the US was a nuclear-armed power with a vast bombing force and huge navy, facing both the USSR, whose internal brutality had somewhat taken the gloss off the notion of Communism as a liberatory movement, and the British, who were attempting to maintain their empire.

For a ruling elite, drawn from Harvard and Yale and filling out the country's new spy agencies, this was carte blanche for fomenting coups in various countries over the next thirty years (Guatemala, Iran, South Vietnam, Chile, Australia), and to stage what became a two-decade war in Indochina. This was the period when the more quasi-religious expressions of exceptionalism didn't need to be invoked, because the idea was being instantiated with bombers, napalm and troops on the ground.

But at its very height, America's self-conception as virtuous also collided with its 'other'. The cultural and social revolution of the 1960s took what had been a minority opinion of the US in the world – that it was a domineering bully, frustrating democracy across the globe, to make it safe for companies like United Fruit Company and Standard Oil – and turned it into mass belief. The protest movements made it impossible to escalate the Vietnam War without tearing the country apart. In 1976, Congress curtailed the powers of spy agencies to destroy governments and assassinate rebel leaders.

The respite was brief. With Reagan's 1980 election, the notion of American specialness came back big-time, a tonic for a nation battered and demoralised by Watergate and

Vietnam. Invasions of Grenada and Panama and the Gulf War in Kuwait were all simple, risk-free operations, restoring US self-belief, albeit in an illusory fashion. When the talk of American exceptionalism died during the Clinton administration, a semi-secret think tank called the Project for the New American Century revived it. The Project, formed in 1997, was composed of figures from both the left and right – former Reagan officials and liberal 'hawks' – all wanting to clean up the tinpot dictators left over from the Cold War and, above all, contest the remorseless rise of China.

The Project bided its time, waiting for the right opportunity. They got it in the early 2000s with the dodgy election of George W Bush and the terrorist attack on the World Trade Center and Pentagon. Among large sections of the US public, there was a marked rise in notions of exceptionalism, the US's special place in the world, and the identification of its interests with the interests of humanity. Mixed in with that was also a dose of pure domination, the energisation of the will-to-power: U-S-A, U-S-A! There had been a bit of that in the Reagan years. In the Clinton era it was expressed by the vast expansion of US consumer prosperity. Now it was back, a roar of pain turned into a shout of triumph.

The nation of Iraq, uninvolved in 9/11, was in the sights of the hawks. Old hands wondered why. They had no problem with the US throwing its weight around, but why attack a secular regime that served as a buffer against the Islamic Republic of Iran?

The Iraq War – and the disastrous occupation of that country and Afghanistan – delivered a smack on the nose to the notion of US exceptionalism that no previous oppositional force had been capable of doing, not even the Vietcong and the North Vietnamese army. After a rapid victory in March–April 2003, the US made a series of mistakes that issued directly from the cartoonish version of exceptionalism which had now infected the country, including much of its intellectually diminished ruling elite. The Iraqi army was disbanded, sending hundreds of thousands of trained men home without jobs; Halliburton and other well-connected multinationals were allowed to determine the course of the occupation for their own profit; and to create a central government free of previous influence, Shi'ite figures were called on, and granted, a constitution enshrining sharia law and Shi'ite control. This half-intended, half-incompetent engineering of social division caused Iraqis to turn on each other and on US troops, and by 2007 the US public was absolutely over it, a sentiment felt across the political and social spectrum. The insistence on forward defence was collapsing, as the body bags and amputee veterans came back week after week. The country was heading into recession from late 2006, and its effects were being felt first in the heartland.

The presence of a liberal elite among backers of the war and occupation convinced many that the whole adventure had been a liberal plot in the first place. By now, the 9/11 conspiracy theories had been mainstreamed. In 2005, Hurricane Katrina and its aftermath had shown US emergency services to be bumbling and incompetent, and pretty much indifferent to the fate of a Black city, New Orleans. The battered and bruised country was getting it from all sides as it crawled towards the 2008 election, where the near-certain winner was saying: 'America isn't uniquely great …'

## Liberally cultish

So what had happened to the 'cult of America', before it made a triumphant return with Donald Trump?

Well, it went in two directions. The first was to the left, reanimating the sort of 'global leadership' liberalism that had been part of American liberalism since the end of World War II. This is the liberalism of the Marshall Plan and the global new deal; of US dominance of global financial and other authorities; of having the United Nations building situated in New York City; of John F Kennedy's 'Camelot' collection of friends, advisors and intellectuals; of the notion that 'the best and brightest' of America could lead the world to a universal prosperity as an alternative to Communism. This didn't turn out so well.

But it was Barack Obama, rising through the ranks after his eye-opening speech to the 2004 Democratic convention, who restored the notion of American greatness to the liberal ideal.

Most likely Obama has never lost a basic scepticism about American claims to a world ethical-historical role, or a mild embarrassment at claims of exceptionalism. But there would appear to be no doubt that in his journey from the outside left – anti-nuclear weapons campaigner, Chicago South Side community activist – to the mainstream, and then to the centre, that he gained an appreciation for the capacity of American power to make things happen, which might be, in the proper hands, something that could turn the world in the right direction.

In Obama's first term there was tremendous excitement that the US could act as, of all things, an agent of multilateralism, negotiation and compromise. During his first presidential campaign, Team Obama made the daring choice for their candidate to make a world tour, and speak in Berlin. By now his crowds inside and outside the US were huge and ecstatic; the swell in Berlin was beyond that. It was a spiritual moment of America rejoining the world, celebrated by the youthful population of a country that had started two world wars and a genocide, and now saw themselves as the global voice of peace:

> The walls between old allies on either side of the Atlantic cannot stand. The walls between the countries with the most and those with the least cannot stand. The walls between races and tribes; natives and immigrants; Christian and Muslim and Jew cannot stand. These now are the walls we must tear down.[18]

But with no substantial reference to America's empire of military bases, no promise of basic structural change in non-military areas – the US stranglehold on the IMF and World Bank, for example – plus the sheen of self-regarding narcissism, the speech was, in Slavoj Žižek's words, 'Obama at his very worst'.[19]

The paradoxical message of this form of globalisation was that the world should be equal and multilateral and proceed through dialogue and consensus – and that the US was the only country with both the power and the founding values to make this happen. Globo-liberalism held contradictory notions in suspension: that nations had the right to self-determination, that cultures differed greatly in their values, and that the moral imperative of a universal set of individual human rights overrode the desire of developing countries to advance by creating a collective value system in the face of an imperialist world system. For an earlier generation of liberals, these unquestionable values had been free markets, property rights, and separation of politics and the public sphere; for the Obama generation, it was the unquestionable belief in identity rights.

It would be easy to call this set of fervent and contradictory beliefs a cult in itself, and later in the book I'll gesture towards that. But there are important features that distinguish it from a genuine cult and mythology, chiefly that it crosses vast numbers of social classes and groups, has a degree of abstract rationality to it, can be argued with by reference to its own contradictions, and its supporters are willing to join the argument and recognise points against it.

This, of course, is the very essence of what the college-educated are trained and shaped to do. And this is part of the asymmetry of our time: that those excluded from this training – with the access to greater economic and social power that it offers – feel that not only is the world against them, but the very practice of rationality itself is. Reason and science were presented throughout the period of modernity, from the nineteenth century on, as a gift to all humanity and the means by which we might arise from poverty and disease. But nothing that happens in our lifetimes will match the deliverance of the polio vaccine or electricity. What persists is reason and science's contribution to luxury – the movie becomes the DVD becomes streaming – and that of comprehensive control. The genuinely new developments, such as ChatGPT, are now greeted with a foreboding that stray remarks about 'luddites' cannot dispel.

Those excluded from the opportunity to wield science and reason – namely the working class trained to routinised labour – are now prodded, pushed, cajoled, calibrated and frequently excluded and cancelled by its operators. For the past four decades those who are the objects of such technical actions have seen their wages, purchasing power and industrial clout diminish, while those doing the pushing and prodding increase not only their economic and political power, but their cultural and social status. This is the great class divide of our time. It was most firmly established with the election and re-election of Barack Obama, where the prodders laid their claim to being the true heirs of the American exceptionalist tradition, albeit implicitly.

The very nature of the other side – the excluded – meant that no response was likely on the same intellectual or abstract plane. The only possible way to resist was to reject reason altogether, and so it was that 'birtherism' not only developed during the Obama years, but spread far beyond what one might have thought was its natural purview of small group racists and fabulators from the South, and close to the Ku Klux Klan (KKK) tradition of white racism, with its horror of miscegenation. Covering the 2010 election, when the Tea Party was at its height, I was continually 'ambushed' by birtherism: a rational discussion of tax policy or the election of the Senate could suddenly veer into a plaintive cry, 'Well, I just think we'll find out when this is all over that he's a Muslim from Kenya.'

What attracted people to such an outlandish view? Such an assertion explained things without having to, as it were, explain how it explained them.

So this was what was happening on the other side to the Obama triumph.

From the moment that Barack Obama took office it was clear that the country was changing. There were multiple

Black faces in the Cabinet and higher echelons, as there were Latinos; and a greater balance between men and women. This was reflected more in popular culture too, where sexuality and gender identity also came into play. The prominently 'out' Ellen DeGeneres dominated the midday TV airwaves; she had previously, in her sitcom, played off the traditional 'is she/isn't she' indeterminacy that had sustained in popular culture for decades. And in 2015, reality TV star Caitlyn Jenner, who was known to millions as 1970s sports star Bruce Jenner, was featured on the cover of *Glamour* magazine as Woman of the Year. The era was one in which progressivism became dominant – a new-found confidence in the assertion of the equality and legitimacy of an ever-wider circle of identities, intersectionalities and itemised wrongs.

Many people were either supportive or indifferent. But there were millions more for whom these new developments were an indication that America, their America, had been lost. Mainstream commentators scoffed at this, pointing out that the country had been divided before: in that small unpleasantness known as the Civil War; and more recently, from the 1930s to the 70s, in the conflicts between the 'New Deal' left and those who considered it to be nothing less than Communism in disguise. What did it matter?

But it did matter to many, especially because it was occurring in the context of a liberal regime trying to de-centre the US from visible and braying world domination.

### The empire cracks up

Barack Obama, the first Black president of the US, was never going to be the commander-in-chief who dismantled the American empire. The hundreds of bases stayed and the notion of all-encompassing war was continued with the CIA's drone counter-terrorism campaign – knowledge-era warfare, light, precise (to a point), not requiring the heavy industrial disaster of actual invasion. With the drone campaign in place to try and blot out stateless radical Islamist groups, Obama thought he might be able to shift the assumption that the US should be front and centre in every world conflict. But he appeared to hope that, with some kind of exceptionalism acting as cover, he could institute a foreign policy that was in contradiction to it. Obama had withdrawn US forces from Iraq (a popular move) and remained in Afghanistan, a policy that many progressives were equivocal about, since their anti-war feelings were blunted somewhat by the mission of preventing the repressive Taliban from recapturing the country. In Libya, in the struggle against Colonel Gaddafi, Obama had lent air support, which made up most of the campaign, with zero US casualties and no boots on the ground. Syria was less successful. The US, with other nations, had been backing insurgent groups for years before the country exploded into civil war.

The chaos put enormous pressure on Obama to take on the exact role for the US that he was trying to avoid: the global moral arbiter, the nation to decide when intervention was required. Obama declared that Assad's use of chemical weapons in the conflict would be a 'red line'; when chemical weapons were indeed used, the consequences of action stayed Obama's hand and his bluff was called. From then on, the US effectively withdrew from Syria, wrapping up its support for some truly nasty players – including Al Qaeda – and re-categorising it as a regional conflict, to be thrashed out by the major locals: Turkey, Iran, Russia and the Arab oil monarchies. In Iran, the US moved steadily forward to make a realistic deal on the Islamic republic's development of nuclear fuel technology. This involved recognising that Iran would do what it wanted to do, but that it could be restrained from doing more – full weapons creation – with the right deal.

The US willingness not to crush an enemy was presented as a gift, and evidence once again of the providence and grace that attended its spirit. But Iran's leaders used the US as a unique enemy in their own domestic politics, and so Obama could not unequivocally suggest that, in the matter of agreements, America stoops to concur without undermining those in Iran who were seeking a deal. So he simply noted that Iran was going to develop uranium processing whatever happened. At that point, in Obama's second term, all hell broke loose. Those on the right could accuse Obama of weakness and traitorousness, and raise the possibility that he was some sort of internationalist double agent, a global Muslim (or not), who had worked his way to the very top, as part of a plan to dismantle US power from its commanding heights.

This was a message whose full success was confined to those who were already hooked on conspiratorial thinking. But many in middle America were disturbed by the spectacle of the US treating a country whose regime they had become accustomed to viewing as a murderous blackmailer as an equal and legitimate player. In the Cold War, this was far more possible for the simple reason that the US, though the leading superpower, was one of two. Avoiding global nuclear war demanded realpolitik and the public granted that to presidents such as Nixon and Johnson. With the US status as the sole superpower, conservative and liberal expectations that the country would be a global moral force returned, even if the ideas differed as to what that morality consisted of.

Given such circumstances, the right would usually be able to capitalise on the notion that the Democrats were inherently weak and lacked faith in American uniqueness. This had elevated Reagan and George W Bush to power, and given a lift to George H W Bush as well. But by 2016, such simple bellicose rhetoric wasn't available to the Republicans. The disaster of Iraq had seen to that. Though it was less of a military/foreign affairs catastrophe than Vietnam, it had extra force by being a repetition of it, and stymied any mainstream Republican trying to revive the Reaganite notion of confidence within and strength without. Trump's challenger from the mainstream Republican right, Ted Cruz, for example, simply couldn't trot out the Reagan mantra – 'let's turn [insurgent country X] into a giant parking lot' – which the neocon right had been repeating during the Iraq disaster.

Donald Trump, or one of his advisors, found the answer, and it was a paradoxical one: don't talk about the moral duty, or the burden of power, or the political objectives that had to be considered in the path to victory; just talk about the victory itself. Trump never used that Latinate term 'victory', but he never shut up about 'winning'. More winning, no nation building. In one of the many self-parodic turns the Trump campaign took, he announced to a rally in 2016 in Albany, New York, that they were going to win so much, they would be 'tired of winning'. The audience cheered to the rafters. This technique was the standard sales pitch: the over-promise was so expansive that it took the potential buyer out of the realm of scepticism and into the land of possibility.

This feint of Trump's marked a new stage in the American story because it offered the irrational belief in the nation's God-given exceptionalism, without the rational justification, religious or secular. Trump's approach introduced to political discourse the sleight-of-hand that he had mastered in becoming a successful businessman and that he 'taught' in the numerous identikit books released under his name, beginning with *The Art of the Deal* (a best-seller written entirely by journalist Tony Schwartz from a few conversations with the dealmaker): a fundamental tenet of this approach was to convince yourself you're a winner – fated by God, destined to succeed – and then forget you had done that.

Now Trump was using this bootstrapping technique to convince the American public to back him for president, while also continuing to teach the public to adopt the method themselves. This latter step was essential, akin to having a receiver capable of picking up a certain signal.

If the US had not been in the condition it found itself in during 2015–16, if one large class was not getting shellacked by the rise of another small class, if that larger social class were not in need of consolation and boosting, then Trump's candidacy would have been that of a bumbling clown. There were examples of that occurring at the time. The head of Starbucks, Howard Schultz, launched an exploratory presidential campaign and was quickly revealed as a delusional narcissist. Billionaire and ex-NY mayor Michael Bloomberg got further into the Democrat primary, but he was equally delusional in his misrecognition of what likely voters might want, and preached the same message of lower taxes and letting genius have its way to create growth. Both crashed and burned.

Trump survived because he was a salesman. While Bloomberg, Schultz and others tried to sell the public on the idea that greatness for Americans came from struggle, from doing, from ingenuity and going beyond yourself, Trump told them exactly the opposite. You were great as you were. It was the country, the leaders who had got it wrong. You were great when you were going to your lunchpail job and coming home to watch your mega-big-screen TV, parking your Jeep in the garage of the home you owned. Trump told people they didn't need to do anything more than that, didn't need to be anything more than that, to be great as an American.

That, as we have seen, was the core of Trump's 'good jobs' offer as his main election pitch. But the whole idea behind it was rolled over into foreign policy. America had to start winning again because America is a winner and winners win – that's what they do. Trump harked back to memories of the Reagan years – of dealing with gnats like Grenada and former clients like Panama's General Noriega – and relied on a convenient amnesia about how the US retained its air of mastery by avoiding any fight that might become real. When suicide bombers killed more than 200 US marines at a base in Lebanon, the Reagan administration withdrew from the country, and the air of invincibility was preserved by sheer sleight-of-hand. What Trump's supporters wanted from a foreign policy was what always sheeted home the supremacy of American power: overwhelming force, through bombs and missile strikes, dealt out to a country of brown people, with zero risk to US personnel.

With Trump, they got them. Or they got one, anyway. In April 2017, the US launched fifty-nine Tomahawk cruise missiles at a Syrian air force base after the Assad government had used chemical weapons in an attack on a rebel Syrian town. Given that the chemical attack had not been against the US, it was hardly Trump's style to launch action, and seemed likely to be a joint chiefs decision pushed on the neophyte president.

The US left Syria and the entire region even faster under Trump than it had under Obama – though this went unmentioned in the right-wing press – to no great protest from Trump's supporters, but no great cheer of triumph either. It's around this time, when it became clear that the promises of the election campaign, the Trumpalooza and return of the 'good jobs', would not materialise, and the turn towards Q and the nakedly cultish aspects of the Trump movement began in earnest.

That Trump could win the presidency of the United States of America in 2016 was evidence that the country was a cult whose combustible elements would flare into fire from time to time. That Trump was defeated in 2020 was evidence that there was a counter-tendency of rationality whose roots could also be traced to the founding revolution. Perhaps one can see American history as a fight between reason and the cult, prior to any left–right division, repeating itself over and over, with different manifestations through centuries. Well, it's a little more complicated than that. But let it serve as an opening remark on a paradox of modernity, that the most powerful nation in the world appears, from the outside, to be also the most insane one; such madness manifested through its claims to reason.

# 3.
# AWAKENING AMERICA

*Pennsylvania, October 2022. Three weeks before midterm election day.*

'Folks, don't let them tell you there aren't tunnels, oh, there are tunnels! I've seen the tunnels! I've been in the tunnels.'

With big country hair and a feisty attitude, Tania Joy Gibson is commanding the main stage. Microphone in hand, she's polemicising, preaching, proselytising about the deep deep state to a crowd that's loving every minute. In cowboy hats and diamante TRUMP caps, they stand, cheer and raise their right hands, Christian witness-style, at just about everything.

It was three and a half weeks before the midterm polling day and everyone was getting their forces out. Especially in Pennsylvania, where everything was to play for.

Gibson gabbles on a million miles a minute: 'Yes, I've been in the tunnels. I was a teen Disney star like Brittany, like Christina, and I know you know it's Disney we grew up with, right, but it's not just the new stuff. Walt Disney was a paedophile and a subversive –'

'Right on!' the crowd yells. 'Yes!' 'Preach!'

Gibson charges on. 'You go back and you look at *The Little Mermaid* and you ask, what's that symbol –'

PAAAAAAAAAAAARP. A huge sound comes from somewhere. Just behind me, almost in my ear, a woman in a cropped haircut and Daniel Boone leathers is blowing a ram's horn. An actual ram's horn.

'What do you think *The Owl House* is about …'

PAAAAAAAAAAAARP.

'Shut up,' a veteran biker type yells. 'Can't hear a goddam thing.'

'Well, ahhhm gonna wrap it up now …' Gibson says as someone starts ringing a bell, a big, old-fashioned, bang-the-sides number.

'Preach, preach …'

'YES!'

PAAAAAAAAAAAARP.

The whole noise of it, the glorious chaos, all bouncing off the corrugated metal walls of the space, as the MC (a thin dude who looks like a 90s art-school rocker) comes back on.

'Tania Joy Gibson! Wasn't she great?'

Welcome to ReAwaken America.

'Twenty cities! Five hundred speakers! We are rolling!' Clay Clark, said 90s rocker, actually a right-wing talk DJ, is revving up the crowd. Awaken America is a slow-burn 'tour' by the sinister-whacko US right, headed by Clark, star of the *Thrivetime Show* podcast. Starting in the west six months ago, it has crossed the US, aimed at the midterms. Pennsylvania is the penultimate stop before it ends on 5 November in

Branson, Missouri, the Ozark Vegas, home of Dollywood and much more.

There must be about 2000 people in this cavernous grey-on-grey auditorium; really a huge garage and a hall of booths and hucksters all in a sports complex called Spooky Nook, with soccer and squash courts, a vast video games arcade and a sad closed food court, Halloween fake cobweb over its shuttered metal grille. At the back, the concession stand is doing a roaring trade, mainly in hot dogs and steaks, yellow liquid cheese gooped all over, the queue snaking all the way back to the entrance where unsmiling black men in uniform run metal detector wands over new arrivals.

On the main stage, a mess of flags and banners, and the drum kit and guitars of the band sit ready for later, the speakers don't stop: Miss Illinois warning about the tunnels, 5G experts, the 'Loose Change' guy arguing that the transgender movement is a transhuman one. The usual mix of Republican dirty tricksters posing as anti-elitists, pastors spruiking Christian nationalism, conspiracy theorists, anti-vaxxers and otherwise uncategorisable obsessives.

'Tour' is a fiction, of course. The sixty or so speakers across two days ('Event starts 8am! Doors open 6am!') aren't on some enormous bus. They fly in from NY/LA/DC every few weeks to whatever hole in the flyover states they're converging on, do their fifteen minutes, maybe sign some merch, then a black car pulls up and takes them to the airport again to get the hell out of there.

There's no printed program and no real support act/headliner structure. It's just one damn thing after another. But that doesn't matter. The crowd can't get enough, whether it's someone announcing the imminent apocalypse or selling vitamin supplements ...

PAAAAAAAAAAAARP. The ram's horn blower is behind my ear now.

'That is really loud,' I mutter.

'Oh, where are you from?' asks a lady in an American-flag shirt and a country string bow tie. Her husband beside her, with his big handlebar moustache, looks ahead intently, not wanting to miss anything.

'Guess,' I say.

'Brooklyn?'

'Australia.'

She looks at me as if I had said Mars. I must have had this sort of exchange half a dozen times over the past few years.

Clay's back on stage. 'Who thinks this election wasn't stolen?' Bewildered silence. 'Ha, I'm kidding! It was stolen, right?' Huge roar.

Pennsylvania is a battleground, *the* battleground now. The Republicans won the state and its twenty electoral college votes in 2016, lost it again in 2020, and now want to take it back. The crucial race is for the Senate seat, held by retiring Republican Pat Toomey, being fought over by aged hoodie-hipster John Fetterman and Trump-backed TV doctor Mehmet Oz. Election-denier Doug Mastriano is running for the governorship, though he has fallen behind and there are three congressional seats that are genuine competitions. They're all Democrat-held – taking them all would get the Republicans 60 per cent of the way along to the five seats they need to flip the House, from this one state alone.

Which is why ReAwaken America is here – to keep up the pressure and energise the base. The Proud Boys will be north of here tomorrow. Ted Cruz is running some sad little bus tour through Ohio and here, making appearances in rural taverns with whoever will stand beside him.

Quite possibly, they have overshot the mark. Where once, pre-Trump, midterm voter turnouts were low, these will surpass the 2018 midterms, if polling is correct, heading towards 72 per cent. That's a rock-up so high that it must extend well beyond the parties' bases (a very variable 30 per cent for the Democrats; a more reliable 20 per cent or so for the Republicans), leading to the paradoxical position that campaigning to your base – stop the steal, abortion with no limits, etc. – will actually repel the moderate and swinging voters now coming to the polls. But of course it's a little more complicated than that.

These roadshows are, first and foremost, an incredible grift, with tickets purchasable only by phone, and only after fifteen minutes of upselling and haggling (a press pass? Fuggedaboutit!). They're sold like cruises, or My Pillow – the highly dubious 'revolutionary pillow system' whose founder Mike Lindell (memoir: *What Are the Odds? From Crack Addict to CEO*) was a stop-the-steal fanatic, a backer of the story about Venezuelan crooked voting machines and a man who said that up to '300 million' people might need to be arrested for voter fraud.[20] In the mini-mall of booths outside the auditorium, people are stocking up on 5G shields, non-vaxx COVID therapies and T-shirts ('Black rifles matter' beside an AR-15 silhouette; 'Trump won!' with the Donald backed by an American eagle; a stars-and-stripes flag made of guns;

Jesus and Trump). Where does the movement start and the grift end?

Suddenly, two announcements: 'Eric Trump is in the building' and 'Please give it up for … Roger Stone!'

Stone, the Penguin himself! Nixon's dirty-tricks guy, then Trump's, the alleged link to WikiLeaks – which both Stone and Trump deny – here he was, white hair, pinstripe suit, slight hump, smirking his way to the microphone. 'He's recently let Jesus into his life,' the announcer adds and a roar goes up.

'We're in a war,' Roger begins, and the crowd loves that. They're less enamoured with the rest of his speech, in which the clash of civilisations is largely expressed through the legal travails of Roger Stone.

'Didn't come to listen to some lawyer,' some handlebar says a few seats away. But Stone gave 'em a bit of red meat, with dark portents about losing America forever, and then the grift again:

'Roger, how much are you paying in legal fees?'

'About thirty grand a month.'

'Let's help this man if we can!'

'I want to thank the Lord for finding me.' Oh Roger. The Nixon tattoo on your back must be laughing blood tears.

But Eric Trump, on stage at the end of the afternoon, I thanked my lucky stars. The headliners had come early, I wouldn't need to come back tomorrow. Slender, bearded, grinning, unfavoured, of course, it's Eric sent out to Podunk, PA, to gee up the halt and lame.

'My dad wants you all to know he loves you very much!' he begins. From there it's a man so desperate for approval that he's willing to ask for it live on stage. 'Let's face it, if my dad were in charge, none of this Ukraine stuff would be happening.'

He has a surprise for us, holding his phone to the camera broadcasting to the big screens up and down the hall. 'DAD' says the caller ID. Yes, it's the Donald.

'I want you to take good care of my boy,' the familiar voice says, all lethal purr.

'Love you, Dad!'

You'd think a patriot crowd wouldn't have much time for princelings. You'd be wrong. These are Christian nationalists, and the Trumps are the holy family. Faces are shining with tears as they gaze up at this failson, live on stage, rotating like donor meat: sweaty, soft, eager to please.

Eric's followed by Dr Joyce, a fundamentalist Christian, PhD chemist and anti-vaxxer, who starts in on a slew of academic papers, losing the audience in seconds. Joyce pulls everything together: white cells, lung membrane, the reptile–mammal division. 'God made us with all we need to resist disease.' The 'jailing' of Dr Fauci is discussed, a crowd favourite. The explicitly satanic nature of vaccination is explored.

This is the first of these things I've been to where some of the speakers were not merely conspiratorial, but actually in the grip of psychosis. The tunnels they obsess over – under Disney, the World Trade Center, Denver airport – are service tunnels. Quite possibly some underhanded stuff has gone on in them, but these folks think they were built by Klaus Schwab and the World Economic Forum to transport abducted children to Jeffrey Epstein's secret island. The ideas of Q are everywhere but mentioned nowhere; some sort of ban has been applied no doubt. The spirit is ecstatic, joyful, voluptuous.

At its root, it is something to do, that gives sense to lives passed by, in a country whose world status is in decline. Long hippie hair on the women, Creedence beards on the men. Thirty different ways of wearing the flag, but *Easy Rider* did it first. Some of these folks want Jesus to return in thunder, and some of them voted for McGovern. Hell, some of them campaigned for him. This is one place where the 1960s ends, the boomers' last tailgate. A long, long trip in the Jefferson Airplane. Talking about the Trilateral Commission in the 70s, and we still are. Just now it's run by shapeshifting lizards. OK, the psychosis might be catching.

Many people stream out with me as Dr Joyce goes into injury time. I buy a guns flag from the concession guy and he makes the mad gesture, finger twirling round the ear, as Dr Joyce talks of frogs and immortalists. I sense a carny type, just running a stand.

'Yeah, lot of crazy stuff today. Stolen election ...'

'Oh man, the election was stolen.' The fake cobweb connection between us breaks. 'You'd have to be crazy not to believe that!'

Tunnels within tunnels, chasing the white rabbit down the hole. Come blow the horn ...

### Requiem for dreams

Had there really been any point in going to another crazy right-wing rally? I asked myself this more than once while on the way out to the middle of nowheresville Pennsylvania, and once or twice more while wandering round the vast sports complex where it was being held – miles and miles out of town, where land is dirt cheap to zero cost, parking is plentiful and the local municipality has been happy to give a permanent land tax holiday for anyone who wants to build anything, anything at all. These sprawling megacentres are all over the US, where families came in their SUVs, determined to make a full day of it – the business of having fun. We've all adopted something of that, a theme-park world – but nothing like the Americans have, with their deconstructed cities, their exuberance everywhere, mainlined by freeways. Once they went downtown to see a movie, went to the boardwalk and had ice-cream, pleasures still integrated into the normal run of life. It was really only in the 1980s that American culture and life began to change in a way that could be said to be described as post-culture and post-life, a world in which every hamburger joint was a McDonald's, every shop was a chain, every downtown was boarded up or demolished and rebuilt as parking garages.

So it was difficult to decide whether what was some sort of Christian, fascist, anti-vaxx rally taking place here, was really a sinister new development in the coming-apart of America or just a ghastly disjuncture, in which the right's obsessiveness had intruded into yet another hitherto neutral space. Had we known the midterm result to come, one could have made a third conclusion: that this crazed fantasia caravan pit stop was entirely suited to a swing-and-a-miss emporium for those who wanted to combine a bit of play with fantasies about superstardom and the chance to overeat.

But we didn't know yet that the right would collapse in the vote. No one did, except Michael Moore – who once again got it exactly right, and whom we, once again, all ignored, distracted by the prospect of the brightly lit right-wing juggernaut bearing down on us.[21]

No one at the ReAwaken America jamboree who was neutral could see it as anything other than a mixture of craze and shonk. But what sort of wider effect did it have? That was the devilish thing to try and work out. It was in this stage of the election – three weeks before polling day – when the right narrative looked triumphant; the idea was that for every ReAwaken America nutter who attended, there were hundreds or thousands more out there who believed enough of this stuff that they would constitute an electoral wave. I wondered, after the election actually occurred and that result came down, if I were now too attracted to the monstrous, exotic and grotesque blooms of the American tree of liberty, to be able to assess the more mundane facts of the nation's political life.

When did it all start to go so wrong? How does a society whose advancements in the areas of science, technology and reason have been so stunning as to take one's breath away, become beset with a war around the most basic idea of what knowledge and truth are? A war in which one side marshals arguments that are essentially medieval, at the very best, and draws on the most lurid mutterings of a century of crackpot conspiracy culture for its authority? And why is the absolute centre of it the US, the country founded on reason?

## Progress stops progressing

Any Australian getting their seniors bus pass today was born sixty or so years ago. In 1958, polio was still a scourge that stalked the land, capable of delivering lifelong paralysis from a swim in a dank pond. Cancer was largely a death sentence, a heart attack was a quick exit, and children with Down's syndrome were locked away in institutions. Twenty-five per cent of urban working populations worked in factories, another twenty-five in repetitive office jobs, another third in routine retail. Five per cent went to college or university, travel was by train, a plane trip was a rarity. A TV set cost many weeks wages, music and movies didn't come in streams, most people ate out at restaurants a few times a year, if at all.

Fast forward to now: diseases like polio are almost entirely a thing of the past, COVID notwithstanding. We don't die of cancer just because we have it. Close to 85 per cent of students complete Year 12, and tertiary courses introduce us to a wide world of ideas and possibilities – extended for the nearly 40 per cent of the workforce who have a university degree or tertiary qualification.[22] There's a lot of factory work still going on, but not much of it in Australia; many jobs are more interesting and creative than they once were. And so on.

Prior to any consideration of how this bounty has been shared out, it is worth stopping to do this simple reflection on how much life has changed, the degree to which enormous amounts of routine necessity have been removed from daily existence, the degree to which a singular idea of the normal has been dethroned for mass acceptance, tolerance and positivity towards people of all different types. It is worth considering the minutiae of everyday life – to take as one random example among many, the work that was required to get someone a photograph of something, twenty-five years ago: the taking, the developing, the delivery; multiple time-consuming actions.

Yet amid all of this, there is a widespread sense, dating from around the late 2000s, that the wonderful march of progress has stopped. For many people, life in the past decade and a half has been shaped by growing inequality and a realisation that the steady extension of the benefits of a modern society had stopped and was now being reversed; that the natural world was now in revolt against the stresses put on it by global society – and yet global society lacked the collective organisation to address this challenge, and the challenge of rebuilding a world where the arrow of inequality was pointing in the other direction, towards less inequality and more opportunity.

Old World nations have resources that their communities can draw on for solidarity and meaning in straitened circumstances, tradition and lifeways that are pre-modern and give a sense of permanence beneath the transience of good times and bad. These traditions can be, and frequently are, abused to try and curb radical action – witness the cries of 'traitors' hurled at British striking workers in early 2023 as they fought for a living wage – but that doesn't detract from their reality as an anchor to life. At the centre of a tradition formed around an ethnic culture, drawing succour from its ancient roots, are notions of consoling fatalism and cross-generational collectivism. Whether our individual lives turned out well or badly, tradition tells us, is a matter of chance, of fate, and is of almost no consequence in the destiny of our people. This is something that not only European cultures can draw on. Indian, Turkish, Arab and Chinese cultures all have this 'reserve store' of meaning. This can be sandwiched together with modernity to create a powerful and compelling national mythos, as is shown by the Chinese Communist Party's deployment of notions of national destiny and purpose in creating a supercharged modern state.

The United States of America does not have that resource. To the outside observer the US is simply bursting with custom and tradition, especially compared to an unassuming culture like Australia's. But these American hallowings and ceremonies are either somewhat isolated customs – such as Thanksgiving – or trace back to the revolution and Declaration of Independence itself, the event which broke with the notion of the legitimacy of received tradition and celebrated humanity's capacity to determine its own circumstances. This gives such non-traditional traditions plenty of expressive energy, but none of the powers of consolation and collectivism that Old World traditions offer.

For those looking for some message that failure and insufficiency in your own life is OK because you are part of something larger, the Fourth of July spectacle of Washington, Jefferson and Lincoln looming over you like a fever dream of Mt Rushmore is no consolation at all. Recourse to the extraordinary American mythos of independence and revolution merely makes you feel more inadequate in a society whose subsequent trajectory – the development of a relentless and unforgiving capitalism – has created a culture which, to some extent, relies on the annihilation of the poor and failed to give a full meaning to the lives of the powerful and rich.

Thus, in place of ancient mythos and the collectivity of a shared ethnic heritage, the US has developed powerful 'myths of modernity' that become the founding stories for the cults of everyday life, and which connect to, and renew, the cult of America itself. Since these myths of modernity usually arise from among the broken and defeated – even if they are then co-opted by the rich and powerful – they are often stories of stolen possibility and promise, of what could have been if one's enemies had not destroyed one. The broken and defeated dream of a single salvation, whether by a great leader or a sudden mass awakening, religious or otherwise.

# 4.
# TWO AMERICAS, BUT NOT THE ONES YOU THINK

In the decade or so after the Civil War, the United States was about as radical a place – in terms of pace of change – as it had or has ever been. 'Reconstruction' kept Northern control over the defeated Confederate states, which were only gradually readmitted to the Union.[23] Full citizenship was extended to African Americans and by 1870 there were African-American congressmen, state politicians and party figures. This outburst of national ethical rationality was a product of the radical transformation of the Civil War itself, which had started as a final measure to preserve the Union, and had become, with the 1863 Emancipation Proclamation, a force for the ending of slavery and the embedding of wider notions of equality – equal treatment of different groups of people – with the Thirteenth and Fourteenth amendments.

The war, and the new Republican Party which had provided the president, Abraham Lincoln, who waged it, came after decades in which the pure republic – innocent of faction and allegedly open to all – had become riven with parties and secret societies. The spread of the Masons was met with an anti-Masonic Party; Catholic secret societies were met with anti-Irish agitation. Gangs formed in the growing cities of the east coast – the Five Points Gang, the Plug Uglies – with rituals and costumes. From them came the 'Know Nothings': anti-immigrant nativists who claimed at least one president (Millard Fillmore), but denied that their organisation even existed. A lot of this was swept away by the simpler, purer recommitment to the American ideal of Lincoln's party.

But as this radical momentum careened on, there were powerful forces dedicated to restoring the corrupt old order. They included Andrew Johnson, who, as vice president, had become president after Lincoln's assassination. Racist and anti-emancipation, Johnson did so much to stymie the social gains of the Civil War that radical Republicans (Johnson was a National Democrat) used the impeachment provisions of the Constitution for the first time to try and remove him (he survived by one vote). Yet he was the least of their worries.

Given the death and misery it has caused, it is ironic that the Ku Klux Klan was founded as a sort of joke, albeit one that was fairly sleazy from the start. With its silly name (a mashup of Greek fraternity names) and white hoods (taken from Spanish secret brotherhoods), the KKK was initially intended as a sort of club of ex-Confederate officers, in the spirit of such joke clubs of the era (usually parodying the Masons). But the time and place of its founding quickly gave it an edge. As Southern ex-officers watched their societies – more willfully archaic and agricultural than the industrialising North – being radically reconstructed, they felt that their world was ending. From being slave societies, the South became one of the most ostensibly progressive and multicultural societies in the world, as hundreds of thousands of slaves became full citizens and sprang immediately into civic organisation. The white response was not political contestation, but terror and intimidation, and the KKK rapidly became the agent of such. Its silly pranks became the nucleus of a social terror strategy in which Black communities were intimidated into civic withdrawal by actual and threatened violence. By the 1870s, reconstruction was over. The implicit racialist beliefs of most white Americans were relied upon to complete the process of de-reconstruction, with the passage of state-level 'Jim Crow' laws separating white and Black communities and subordinating the latter. In 1896 the Supreme Court shamefully confirmed such laws in the *Plessy v Ferguson* case.

By then, the KKK had been operating for decades and had spread to the North as well. It had become a general, floating brotherhood of white Protestant supremacy, taking up in the process all the obsessions of the original Know Nothings. To its vicious anti-Black stance, it added the notion that Catholics were organised from the Vatican, in a vast global conspiracy. It soon took on the anti-Semitism that had arisen in Europe in the 1870s, as significant numbers of Jews began to arrive as immigrants. Indeed, the KKK began to display the behaviour that would come to be distinctive in American conspiracy: a capacity to accrete multiple conspiracies and suspicions to an initial single obsession and create a vast and complex web of paranoia.

They had much fertile ground. The United States in which they found themselves was bounding ahead. After the Civil War, wage-based capitalism – far more productive than slavery – spread across the whole nation. The Republicans had passed Bills that pushed ahead with a national railroad and a public university system, and the resolution of the slavery issue had opened the frontier to rapid expansion (and the vast violence that went with it). The American tilt towards practicality and innovation that has been present since the Revolution brought forth a slew of inventions and discoveries that founded huge industries, such as modern steel production and the oil and petrol/gasoline industry. The millions of immigrants were the raw material for this new boom; desperate, exploited, poorly paid, they built cities and industries. By the 1870s, the US was catching up to Great Britain, the industrial behemoth. By the 1880s, it had surpassed it. The sense of what America was had changed utterly. The last ideas of the modest agrarian republic, a place made of *cincinnati* (farmers like the Roman general Cincinnatus, who left his farm to command the empire and save the city, and then returned to his farm, a conception which gave its name to a midwestern city) was long gone. The American self-image of practicality and know-how was now attached to accumulation, wealth and production for sale, something that had been far less dominant in the pre-war era. The 'Colossus' was born.

But in this period – known as the Gilded Age for the sudden and unfamiliar opulence appearing everywhere – something else was born. Like every society, the US always had inequality – and of course nothing is unequal like a slave plantation – but with the post–Civil War rise of industry, fortunes ballooned and inequality became vertiginous. This was due not only to the roar of factories and innovation, but to a new American invention, the limited company. This was a startlingly paradoxical innovation, created in New York in 1811, and soon copied by other states. In an era of debtors' prisons, the 'Ltd.' said you could start an enterprise, attract investors, see it go belly-up ... and not have to pay them back!

Such innovations reversed the relationship between traditional religious morality and capitalism. The latter came to the centre of American life – and supercharged investment, stockmarkets and innovation. The tycoons of the Gilded Age, such as Andrew Carnegie and John D Rockefeller, were multi-millionaires, but with the purchasing power of multi-billionaires today. They mercilessly used the endless supply of immigrant labour to hold wages down to starvation level, and used private armies to maim and kill those who sought to strike for better conditions. America's cities became vast and the country became an urban nation with endless miles of cheap tenements and crowded neighbourhoods.

These conditions would produce a political response with the rise of the Populist and then Progressive movements. Over several decades these radical and reforming parties forced government to take a role in relief for the poor, in education and in opportunity, in making it possible for working people to organise. But it also produced the first honest to God American religious–political cult. They came from the east with the great frontier migration in columns of horses, with their own flags, a leader they believed to be the Messiah, their own Holy Book and a story about lost gold plates. They were the Mormons.

### Go west, young Mormon

Joseph Smith was a mystic preacher in New York, who announced in 1830 that the angel Moroni had come down from heaven and given him twelve gold plates announcing the scriptures and a new vision of the world. The plates, which, translated, became *The Book of Mormon*, announced that Smith himself was the Messiah, that the United States was the Holy Land of scripture, that Native Americans were the twelve lost tribes of Israel, and that Smith and his followers should trek west to build Zion, the promised land.

The Mormons were entire and of themselves as they set out in the 1830s and 40s to the newly marked-out Utah Territory – part of the wide gap between the east and California, and above what was still the northern part of Mexico, where Colorado is now. Though they were Americans by scripture – scripture being *The Book of Mormon* – they did not see themselves as US citizens, but creators of a new realm. Consequently they clashed with those along the way and with neighbouring settlements when they got there, and with each other as the movement split into sects.

But with the post–Civil War consolidation of the US across the breadth of North America, the Mormons couldn't stay separate and they were effectively incorporated into the US proper. This had one major problem: their practice of polygamy (which they had claimed to adopt for reasons of maximising their own 'tribe', but which seemed more to do with the Mormon elders wishing to have a harem). Some Supreme Court cases in the 1870s decisively established that the practice was not protected by the First Amendment freedom of religion provision, prompting a further split, with one faction going underground.

Those that didn't go underground took the very opposite path, one which was to have major consequences. Choosing worldliness and integration, they dived deep into the American mainstream and rapidly became a current in American life. There was much that was attractive about their religion – which they considered to be the true Christianity – in its collective worship, close community and successful abstemiousness (banning not only alcohol and tobacco, but coffee, tea and sweet stimulants). Where the old small-town sense of community was being lost, Mormonism offered a constructed version of it. From their base in the city that they built beside Utah's Great Salt Lake, Mormon missionaries went out to all corners of the US.

They were part of a rich conversation. Christian sects, and quasi-Christians such as the Quakers, had never stopped trying to spread their various messages (tellingly, proselytising had been suspended for the duration of the War of Independence; and Manhattan had had a ban on such activities from the start, which has determined New York City's character to this day). In the 1820s, the Transcendentalist movement (combining theology, nature and German philosophy of the self), had emerged from Harvard and spread throughout New England and beyond. But here's what makes the Mormons so important in this story. All of these sects and cults sought to simplify their message, to find the essence of God and the world, turning away from complex cosmology. The Mormons too had a sensible, practical way of organising everyday life, which gave one a rich and loving community, and maximised health, self-discipline and focus. Yet Mormonism was bolstered by a whacky set of stories straight out of a children's fantasy or a lunatic's babblings. Twelve gold plates from an angel? You couldn't drink wine, but you could have four wives? After death, everyone got their own planet?[24] *And it didn't matter at all.* They grew and grew, and their legions of new followers dragged the crazy ideas with them.

Maybe it was the frontier and a sense that anything was possible. Maybe it was the absence of an older country's actual myths that everyone knows to be crazy, such as King Arthur, the sword in the stone and the lady in the lake. But after the wild success of the Mormons something became clear to anyone making a movement in the US: when in doubt, make it crazier.

Thus, through the second half of the nineteenth century, the US had all the things that were popping up elsewhere in the world: revival religious caravans, small sects, movements of personal improvement, socialist communes – thousands of socialist communes! The space was wide open for them, and not just the rolling acres. It was the imaginative space that was open, a space of creativity that existed 'before' market forces, in a pure state, but whose ideas could then be supercharged with those forces.

Some ideas were tragic, some absurd. In Michigan, a semi-quack doctor took over a sanatorium for the growing numbers of people with physical debilitation from a variety of bodily and mental causes. The doctor's weirdo mix of treatments included a ban on masturbation and spicy foods, yoghurt enemas and an examination of one's own faeces to see if it had symmetry and lightness. What happened to this crazy set-up? Well, you probably had some of it for breakfast. This was Dr John Harvey Kellogg, whose health regime did not survive, but whose eponymous corn flakes (actually created by his brother) conquered the world.

On the other hand, the Quakers were so appalled by the degrading and crimogenic conditions of English prisons that they promoted the Panopticon – a prison divided in such a way that inmates understood that they could be watched at any moment without knowing it – so that isolated prisoners would relate only to God, and thereby be cured of sin. This new thing, the 'penitent-iary', was seen as pretty awful, even at the time. Charles Dickens famously denounced it when touring the US.[25] But it spread throughout the US, at the same time as the God it relied on to relate to prisoners died away for many of the criminal class, or became a cipher. By the mid-twentieth century the penitentiary's enforced solitude had become a device of exquisite existential torture, worse than any common pit. As religious notions of Hell and eternal punishment receded, the American state responded by locating it in the prisons, with sentences of surreal length – some of which were hundreds of years. The do-gooders had opened an abyss in the heart of humanity. Making progress can be a tricky thing.

As the Gilded Age rose and made some people vastly rich and many more people poor, the rational and direct political response was the Populist movement, which stirred people up to oppose both major parties for being unresponsive to their needs and, in the 1890s, forced through a whole series of political changes that shaped the distinctive US system of today.[26] These changes included public 'primary' elections for party candidates – a measure to ensure that candidacies would not be decided in smoke-filled rooms.

But the Populist movement had, within and without it, complex and paranoid mythologies about the gold-standard money system, the Federal Reserve, who controlled credit, the opening of the west, and whether 'bimetallism' – introducing silver as an additional currency of reserve alongside capital-constricting gold, to expand the money supply – was a great leap forward or an invention of the devil. It may even have made an appearance of sorts in *The Wonderful Wizard of Oz*, published in 1900 ('follow the yellow brick road').

By the first decade of the twentieth century, there was every political cult, secret society, brotherhood and esoteric society you wanted.

Everyone was doing it. Americans had managed to push back against the brutal imposition of segregation; intellectual leaders such as W E B Du Bois and George Washington Carver painstakingly developed campaigns, but who really moved people? Marcus Garvey, a Jamaican activist, landed in New York in 1916 with a plan for African Americans to return to Africa. Brilliant, manic, visionary and delusional all at once, Garvey founded a movement that proposed what seemed impossible, but crucially set free the imagination about what was possible for Black Americans. The gradualist approach of Du Bois and others seemed overly cautious by comparison.

In the 1920s, Garvey was followed by Wallace Fard Muhammad, who established the Nation of Islam in Detroit in 1930. His group's mythology suggested that Black people had a special cosmic origin and were vastly superior to whites – an 'ice people' who were incapable of true feeling or greatness. As before, the fantasy gave the reality a fillip: Fard Muhammad encouraged Black people to dress like American white Anglo-Saxon Protestants – with suit, white shirt and bow tie (the WASPS now dress fauxletarian; the Nation of Islam has maintained the dress code) – and to start their own businesses. The myth of ancient roots – traced back to the Egyptians, posited, reasonably enough, as the African precursors of the Greeks – gave people the sense of glorious possibility they needed to unbend themselves from the relentless hail of racial hatred and disdain.

### Here come the political machines

While all this was going on, there was also the tremendous development of the two main political parties – the Republicans and the Democrats – into the dominating right and left forces we have today. You could pretty much date the mainstream right and left in the US from either the 1896 or 1912 elections, with a final transitional period in between.

In 1896, Republican William McKinley defeated Democrat William Jennings Bryan for the White House. Bryan has been rendered as a fool in history because he was the lawyer for the party that brought suit against a Tennessee teacher for teaching the theory of evolution, in the *Scopes Monkey Trial* of 1925. But in 1896, he was a dashing hero to millions, a self-proclaimed socialist who raged against the iniquity of the Gilded Age. McKinley's victory ended the Democrats' brief romance with socialism. However, McKinley was assassinated only two years later, in 1898, by an anarchist bomb. His VP, Theodore Roosevelt, became president.

Roosevelt was the last Republican who was a mixture of left and right, introducing pensions, some union organising rights, public education, national parks and a first attempt at socialised health care. But in 1908, his VP and successor, William Howard Taft, broke Teddy's left–right compromise, and his heart, and sided with the party's right, the 'business Republicans'. In 1912, Roosevelt ran against Taft, on the Progressive Party ticket, pushing a full left-leaning slate. His run split the vote and the Democrat Woodrow Wilson was elected. He promptly took over a lot of Roosevelt's Progressive Party program.

Formerly radical and federal, the Republican Party became the party of business. The formerly states-rights Democrats became the party of government action for social improvement. Away the twentieth century went.

For the next half century the Republicans were a largely rational centre-right political party (by US measures). They held the White House through the 1920s and again in the 50s, even as the decades from the 30s to the 70s were dominated by New Deal (Democrat) politics. The New Deal Democrats proposed smaller government, lighter taxes, were probably better on race than the Southern-heavy Democrats and functioned as a loyal opposition. The Republicans did a lot of work to exclude the hard-right elements whose cultish politics had started to develop in the 30s. Paranoid politics, such as the obsessive notion that the mild civil rights demands of Black movements were being driven by communists, was as likely to come from the Democrats as the Republicans.

America's first Red Scare began at the end of World War I. The Bolshevik Revolution in Russia had electrified the world in 1917 and showed the large and radical working-class movement what was possible. Across the world, the end of the war had brought millions of troops home, smack bang into the 1919 post-war mini-depression. Strikes shook the West, and the US was no exception, with whole cities consumed by general strikes and a new universal union – the Industrial Workers of the World – making great gains. State and federal governments cracked down hard with a wave of arrests, repressive new laws, faked charges and extra-judicial executions of union leaders – all assisted by company-hired thugs. By 1921, the union had been broken, the economy was growing again, and radical energies were dispersed. Warren Harding – the corrupt Republican good ole boy, who usually appears at the top of 'worst president' lists – pardoned many anti-war and socialist activists.

In 1922, the FBI was formed. J Edgar Hoover took control of it soon after and ran it for a half century. He used it as a personal agency, amassing vast files capable of blackmailing politicians, judges and activists and disrupting domestic political groups. The Communist Party of the USA was formed, a hard-edged, Moscow-affiliated outfit. And the Ku Klux Klan revived, a response to the 'great migration northward', as African Americans from the southern states responded to the desperate need for labour in northern factories and the new wave of violent, racist hanging and burning murders – the word 'lynchings' rather softens the horror of them – headed to Kansas City, Detroit and Chicago.

The KKK got ownership of the 'paranoid style' of American politics. Its revival in the 1920s created much of the sinister political theatre for which it has been remembered in popular culture – the full hoods and burning crosses thing. By then, its rollcall of enemies was substantial: Southern Europeans, Mexicans, bohemians, newly independent women, socialists, trade unionists; Catholics had fallen behind somewhat, Jews came to the forefront. This was part of the wave of anti-Semitism that would engulf the West in the inter-war period, and it saw the creation of what one might call the 'complex American conspiracy': smart, rich, well-connected Jews were behind the rise of Blacks, who were regarded as insufficiently intelligent to organise themselves.

The conspiracy became ever more complex as new groups were added to the KKK's list of enemies. Was this a global Jewish conspiracy, using the communists as a front, to flood good white societies with Catholics, Slavs and Blacks? Or was it a vast Catholic operation run from the Vatican, with communism as its false front in the working class, operated by the Jews?

The KKK and similar groups gained a huge following in the 20s as community boundaries started to break down. The automobile changed the neighbourhood character of big cities, hitherto carved up by ethnicity; radio and films opened new worlds. Jazz was pure excitement – a brilliant, kinetic sound splash uniting body and mind – and Black players did it best of all, so white kids started going 'slumming', heading to clubs in Harlem and other African American areas for the good stuff. Woodrow Wilson had used World War I to pioneer a new doctrine of internationalism, and half of his famous 'fourteen points' for a post-war world were taken from Bolshevik demands issued in 1917. The Republicans may have prevented the US from joining the League of Nations, but it had still been established, and was slowly promulgating a notion of universal human rights. The world seemed to be going crazy and the KKK had the answers.

The 1929 stockmarket crash, and the resulting Great Depression, sent politics scattering and caused a substantial regrouping. As Republican President Herbert Hoover responded to the Depression with austerity measures (thus deepening it), the rich were doing okay, the banks were made of marble (as the Woody Guthrie song went) and the poor were in the wind, which was blowing up the Dust Bowl in the Midwest. Support for socialism and communism surged, and many recruits were from those who had previously been blaming their problems on the Jews and the Vatican.

The rapid radicalisation caught the Democrats on the hop, and in 1932 their candidate Franklin Delano Roosevelt (FDR), responded by taking on most of the program of the Progressive Party. The Progressives (a European-style social democratic party) had been founded by Theodore Roosevelt for his third-party presidential run in 1912, drawing on numerous radical state groups. Believing that a frontier society would never support a mass socialist movement, the Progressives pushed for the idea of active government in partnership with unions and the private sector to: institute public health care, organising rights and aged and disability pensions; expand public education; impose campaign funding limits and much more.

In 1932 the Progressives' greatest success was practically their final act. FDR took over their program, created the 'New Deal', identified the Democrats with it, and by the 1940s the Progressives had dissolved entirely. FDR and his left-wing 'brains trust' not only introduced a radical program, they also changed the way Americans thought about government. In his State of the Union address of 1941, ahead of the war he was about to take America into, FDR named the American spirit and cause as that of 'four freedoms': freedom to speak, freedom to worship, freedom from want and freedom from fear. The *Saturday Evening Post* cover artist Norman Rockwell did a four-part series of these freedoms, and it is the third, 'freedom from want', that became the most famous: depicting a large (white) family sitting down to a Thanksgiving dinner, the mother placing the roast turkey on a table groaning with food. This, millions felt, was what

America was about, a community grounded in sufficiency, just reward for labour yielding forth the fruits of the earth.

The only trouble with this was, there was nothing 'American' about it at all. FDR had performed an enormous sleight-of-hand and sold it as a vision for the world (and a justification for the US to go to war). There is no guarantee of 'freedom from' any life circumstance in the Constitution or its tradition. It is entirely geared to 'freedom from' imposition by the state. Free speech is freedom from laws that would prevent one speaking; freedom from unreasonable search and seizure (the Fourth Amendment) is freedom from capricious police actions, and so on. Nowhere does the Constitution guarantee that you have a right not to starve, or live in perpetual fear that you might starve. These are what we call 'positive' freedoms, based on the idea that 'negative' freedoms – those that restrain the state – are pointless if you don't have the wherewithal to be a citizen and a human: to be able to speak, worship, organise, etc. By applying the term 'freedom', and switching the polarities 'to' and 'from', Roosevelt persuaded millions that a European-style quasi-socialist program was the essence of America! Rockwell, a progressive (his late career would suffer for his opposition to the Vietnam War), did the rest.[27]

This notion of what America was, remained dominant until the 1970s, when the crises of the state and economy allowed Ronald Reagan to offer an alternative mantra: 'Government is not the solution to our problem, government is the problem.'[28]

During the New Deal heyday, the conspiratorial right didn't go away. It simply had its energy stolen. The most visible leader of the American right was Charles Lindbergh, the hero who had flown the Atlantic, a mega-celebrity of newsreels, radio and magazines. But he could get nowhere with his 'America First' movement. Such mythical conspiracies offer a sense of community, imbued with purpose, but only by the myth itself. The solutions are magical. When a rational politics can offer the same sense of real community through social reconstruction, people flock to it.

Still, the era showed that Americans love clubs, networks and brotherhoods, and the secret rituals that go with them. From the late 1800s through to World War I, organisations of men (largely businessmen) were created in what appears to be a secular response to the decline of church sects, and the need for some form of in-group gathering. Rotary, the Kiwanis, the Shriners, the Loyal Order of Moose(!) are among the most famous. They spread nationally and globally after World War I, but hundreds like them sprung up in each city. Their stated purpose was 'service', fundraising for hospitals and other facilities, which they did. But this also gave a sort of alibi for the other side of the clubs, which was to allow businessmen, and their wives as an auxiliary, to relax from a public mode of seriousness in a private setting. The Kiwanis and the Shriners adopted special clothes – such as the Shriners' distinctive red fez – much of it a gentle parody of Masonic rituals (of which many were also members). They staged elaborately decorated fancy-dress balls, making costume parties a major cultural activity for the middle-class from World War I to the 1960s.

The rise and popularity of these clubs, and the culture that arose from them, show us that the US had both a talent for, and a desperate need to, invent rituals, often giving them a retroactive gloss. From the 1920s, with the creation of a vast culture industry covering movies, radio, popular music, magazines and pulps, so far as popular culture myth went, the US became the workshop of the world. Cowboys had originally been gangsters driven out of cities after the Civil War; heading West, they maintained their urban styling and dandyism, a performative swagger. As the frontier closed, a few, such as Wyatt Earp, ended up in Hollywood, wrangling horses for the movies, and feeding their stories into the script machine. Modern gangsters, emerging during the 1920s, were written up by urban sociologists, whose writings were used by scriptwriters such as Ben Hecht, who created *Scarface* – which every gangster then modelled himself on.

### Twelve steps to self

But the most influential of such movements in this interwar period were those that might have seemed the most unlikely to shape the whole culture. In 1935, Bill Wilson, a Wall Street broker who had ruined his career with alcoholism, was persuaded to join a Protestant activist sect, the Oxford Group (it would later become the Moral Rearmament movement), as a way of curing his addiction. That didn't work, but when Wilson combined a medical notion of alcoholism with a generalised religious model of God and the notion of conversion (his first 'convert' was an Akron doctor named Bob Smith) he had created a formula which seemed to have a much greater success than older, religiously bound, temperance movements. Wilson and Smith began organising circles of alcoholics to share their experiences and to surrender their moral will to God, 'however they understood him'. This essentially made 'God' a vanishing point of authority, with no contact; a form of surrender acceptable to agnostics and even atheists.

This generalised notion of God had become increasingly well known in America in the first twenty years of the twentieth century, with the spread of eastern religions and their variants into the West. In the 1900s, the movement that would claim the greatest share of many such adherents was Theosophy, founded by a Russian immigrant, Madame Blavatsky. It gained hundreds of thousands of followers with a message that all gods were one, and religion and science expressed a universal principle of the sacred.

As Wilson and Smith's Alcoholics Anonymous (AA) circles spread throughout the US, the founders elaborated on what would become the famous Twelve Step Program, and eventually gained millions of members. The shift that the founding and wild success of AA represented was both a signpost in US culture and a creator of the culture that was to come, for it centred the alcoholic's recovery on an internal struggle by one part of the self against the other, with the assistance of those outside. This was the Puritan struggle against doubt and temptation secularised, and then fused with twentieth-century psychology, drawing in aspects of psychoanalysis. It introduced much of the language of complex subjectivity – notions of avoidance, denial, repression, of the addiction model of desire – to mass culture.

When, in the 1980s, the culture collapsed into Reaganism and remorse, it was the addiction model, and the 'X Anonymous' treatment model, that became not only the central way of treating addiction but the central model of selfhood altogether. Indeed, by the 1990s, it had become a version of the 'hero's journey'. This was the fantastically influential idea of anthropologist Joseph Campbell, that a single hero myth lay at the root of most cultures – whereby a hero, who is 'out of step' in their own society, is challenged to save that society as it comes under threat, their role revealed to them by an older mentor, who gives them a magical object; completing the challenge reveals to the hero their essential role at the centre of their own culture. Circulated in Hollywood by *Taxi Driver* screenwriter Paul Schrader, it was then repurposed by George Lucas to create the literal myth of *Star Wars*, thus returning an affirmative frontier mythology fused with technology to the centre of American culture. The bloated, hyperconsumptive America of the 1990s saw its salvation in the individual journey back from wastedom of its celebrities and artists. They were saving America by saving themselves; rehab – for alcohol, drugs, eating, not-eating, sex, etc. – became the surplus society's version of a religious retreat.

What came before that, between the straitlaced world of the 1950s and the hangover of the 80s was, of course, the party of the 1960s and 70s. So much happened in the 60s that it really needs its own book, but the simplest possible characterisation of it would be around the manifested desire for a return to nature: nature without – the wilderness – and nature within – the self uncorrupted by the shaping and demands of civilisation. This tendency is as old as urban civilisation itself, and in the eighteenth century Jean-Jacques Rousseau brought the idea to the centre of what we call the 'radical enlightenment', arguing that oppression was not merely a matter of tyrants and absolute power, but of power itself, and the corrupting effects of civilisation.

There was more than a touch of this spirit in the American Revolution. The Americans may have seen the ability to conduct commerce as a right that the Crown was obstructing; but the notion of endlessly accumulated wealth was not central to their vision. In the South, it was felt that the household-based slave plantation economy would act as a bulwark *against* the new country being drawn into a world of big cities and the rule of money – there was very little that a slave owner with an estate needed to actually ever buy, as opposed to being made at home – with the classical world being the model. After all, slaves had been essential to their civilisation too.

Indeed, though the political right would like to identify the American project with capitalism, it was only after the Civil War that such an identification became true. Capitalism – the idea that accumulation should be unlimited and should determine all other social relations – was not something that most Americans would have recognised as true for much of the nineteenth century. Instead, the new country, with its endless supply of new land – made possible by the steady dispossession of Native Americans – became a destination for Europeans wanting to create ideal societies from scratch, having found that impossible in the Old World. Some were purely and literally religious, such as the Amish or Mennonites, who had come to America so as to not be subject to military service in Germany. Settling in Ohio and Pennsylvania, these extreme Protestants lived, and live, by the Bible; their interpretation of which steers their selective adoption of new technologies – and the creation of new communities, as old communities split over differing forms of such interpretation. Seen as backward due to their archaic dress and habits, their method of managing social change – debating the pros and cons of new technologies (albeit through scriptural interpretation) – is in some ways a more sophisticated approach to the matter than our approach of letting capitalism decide.

Others who continued the country's Puritan origins did so in a more worked-upon fashion, such as the Shakers – a form of Quakerism which celebrated ecstatic trance worship rather than silence ('shaking Quakers'). The Shakers would have grown in vast number had they not been celibate, childless and reliant on conversion – as can be seen from the example of the Mormons, who took a rather different approach. The Oneida communes that spread from upstate New York in the 1840s also varied from both the Shakers and the Mormons, in declaring that anyone could have sexual relationships with anyone else, and that such was the ultimate Christian resistance to possessiveness and worldliness. These experiments were part of an archipelago of such communities across the Midwest, which included numerous similar societies that were fully secular in their beliefs. Brook Farm was the most famous, founded on the principles of transcendentalism elaborated by Ralph Waldo Emerson and Henry David Thoreau, but there were dozens of others, often influenced by the utopian French socialist Charles Fourier, who advocated communities of two thousand, led by a wise elect.

It would be an exaggeration to say that such communities formed any sort of dominant presence in the expanding republic. But nor were they a rarity. In the nineteenth century, the whole country was being formed by the creation of communities from nothing. Amid the violence of ongoing dispossession, most Americans and new immigrants thought of themselves as part of something larger, but also immediate and face-to-face. Though some, such as the Oneida community, scandalised many, there was nothing odd about the idea of a community living by a certain rule.

Yet this America would not only start to falter by the 1880s, it would largely disappear from the memory of what the country had been. Many of the communities were victims of the internal contradictions of utopianism: in pursuit of a perfected life in harmony with nature, they became rule-bound autocratic cults, from which all but the most stalwart departed. Around them, the country's modernisation made the idea of a bucolic free space, outside of a state order, near impossible. The rise of the first consumer society and its key invention – the mail-order catalogue – made the blandishments of the world too tempting. Going further west was not viable: beyond the Mississippi, the land became arid, and community small farming impossible.

By the 1880s, America, the colossus, sprawled across the continent. On its vast rail network, one could ride among the thousand points of the world's new powerhouse, taking work, settling or moving on, alone, making and losing companions along the way. A new type of American, a new type of person, was emerging. Someone who found their life as an individual among all this, tracing their own path, bearing its great risk – loneliness and anomie – for a chance at its great possibilities. This enormous potentiality was given literary form in the work of Walt Whitman.

This is the America we recognise as the one that captivated the world's imagination, from the Western myth of sprawling lawless country, to the towering cities made vast and anonymous by the new 'skyscrapers' rising in Chicago, Buffalo and New York. Within it would bloom its exact opposite, a radical return to nature, the seeds blown in from Europe.

# 5.
# COUNTERCULTS AND THE CULT OF PROGRESSIVISM

In 1916, the German immigrant William Pester arrived in California, and a revolution in American life had its very modest beginnings. Pester was a follower of the German *Lebensreform*, a movement that had started in the 1860s as a return to nature. Pester set himself up in Palm Springs – then a desert outpost – grew his hair and beard to Jesus-length, and lived a minimal life playing guitar, extolling the virtues of raw fruits and vegetables and selling postcards to curious tourists who started to come in droves from Los Angeles. By the 1920s, he had a following, and by the 30s they had spread through the country. Known as 'Nature Boys', they were a small but familiar fixture of the era. In the 1940s, they became very famous when one of their number, eden ahbez (he preferred the lower case), wrote the instant classic song 'Nature Boy' about a fellow practitioner, Gypsy Boots, who had established the first health food store in Los Angeles, and combined fruit with the then obscure food yoghurt to create the smoothie. 'Nature Boy' was a smash hit, ahbez became a brief fixture on early TV – he rode his bike onto the set of a talk show sponsored by an oil company; possibly the first such protest – and numbers of the Nature Boys swelled, especially in and around San Francisco.

In the 1950s they would have contact of a sort with the Beatniks who had travelled west from New York, and in the 60s these two countercultural strands would combine, and become mass cultural with the rise of the 'hippies' – essentially, Nature Boys who were hip. The music was harder-edged, the lifestyle was urban and inner-city, and drugs took the place of nature for ecstatic experience. This would in turn beget the 'counterculture', returning to the country from the city to start communes.

The Nature Boys' hippie influence on everyday life in the US was vast. The country in 1965 was clean-cut. By 1970, millions of men were wearing their hair beneath their shoulders, women's fashion was dominated by flowing folky dresses, people went barefoot and rock music festivals (such as the epoch-defining mudbath of Woodstock in 1969) became a thing. This was more than a fad. By the 1980s, men's hair would be returning to a shorter length, and the punk and new wave movements would usher in a change of presentation. But by then, there was a health food store on every street, yoga was a mainstream activity, non-Western medicine was becoming a go-to resource. The 'New Age' movement was spreading, psychedelic drug use was widespread, and the sexual revolution had established unbounded sensuality as at the centre of a happy life. Much of this would survive the political counter-revolution of the 80s and simply be incorporated into the lifestyle of a society that had given up on the brief effort to transform capitalism, and had now made its accommodations with it. Whatever effect it has had, the Nature Boys must count as one of the most successful cults of all time, and a model for a more general process of US society – the sudden mass distribution of an obsessive idea into general commerce. This is especially so in the adoption in the 1960s and 1970s of cybernetic and network theories of human sociality, which would lead – via the movements such as Stewart Brand's *Whole Earth Catalogue* of 1970 – to a hippie 'infusion' into computing, which would produce the Apple and subsequent personal computers that would then transform our lives.

Their success might be partly attributed to the fact that they were largely left alone in the 1940s and 50s, because they were considered to be harmless, and also because they were white. Corresponding Black movements, such as the 'hip' movement around bebop jazz, got far harsher treatment. But it was also because much of the 50s was consumed with another and greater enemy within: the threat of communism, its proponents directing a vast conspiratorial movement across the US.

The Communist movement and membership of the Communist Party of the USA had grown enormously during World War II, when the USSR was an ally of the US, and the news media and Hollywood mounted a huge propaganda effort on its behalf. But the Cold War began in the 1940s, China fell to the Communists in 1949, and the global movement began speaking of world revolution. A Congress subcommittee, the House Un-American Activities Committee, began investigating many people – such as Hollywood screenwriters – who had hitherto been praised for their radicalism, and were now deemed to have been what was bitterly called 'premature fascists'. In the 30s, many progressives and intellectuals had joined the party or been 'fellow travellers'. A handful (in positions of some power) had probably spied for the USSR in minor ways. From this, the new Wisconsin senator Joseph McCarthy spun an elaborate conspiracy, detailing an ever-changing number of Communists in the State Department, Hollywood, the army, the *New York Times*.

The 'Red Scare' was American paranoia at its finest, and it fused with a wider air of unease that ran throughout the country, beneath its sunny post-war surface. *Film noir* (the product of German Expressionists meeting Hollywood) conjured up this sinister air of a society that had been very rapidly modernised and alienated by World War II. Subsequent writers such as James Ellroy have captured its other aspects well: a renewed racism against Black and Latino people as industrial work brought them into the cities and the civil rights movement fought for their equality; the persecution and entrapment of homosexual men, in a world that the war had loosened up; and a foreboding about technological futures stirred up by the appearance of the atomic bomb in 1945 and the development of a Soviet version by 1949.

This quickly coalesced into the UFO hysteria, a cult as American as Mormonism, and that shared some features with it. Arising from the increased presence of test flights, A-bomb tests and other aerial phenomena from Air Force facilities in the Nevada and southwest deserts, and taken up by the science-fiction magazines, it managed to combine gnostic ideas of a secret truth of the universe, imparted by ethereal messengers, with a faith in technology as a form of deliverance and the idea that such aliens would naturally choose the US as the nation to contact. In Utah, hundreds of thousands of people believed that angels walked among them; in Nevada, it was humanoid figures descending from saucer-shaped objects. Around this, a vast cult of knowledge built up, in which, pre-internet, people could spend their lives pursuing snippets of information to find conclusive proof, not only that aliens were among us, but that the US government was hiding the fact.

## The gnosis will see you now

The UFO cult gave a cosmic form to what was an emerging cult also distinctive to the US among the advanced countries, 'political gnosticism'. All modern societies had dark forebodings about 'deep states' and they were often elaborate. But they were also essentially medieval in form, and the answer to their bedevilment was usually simple; it was usually to kill the Jews. In the US, political gnosticism put a premium on the act of knowing itself, of not being fooled by the conspiracy and of mapping it out.

There was much raw material. World War II had caused the reorgansiation of the US into a total war society in which government, military, science and industry were fused together in a vast operating system governing daily life. The newly formed CIA and an expanded FBI were operating beyond any notion of government accountability that the Constitution might have dictated. The texture of everyday life was being changed with new technology: the television, transistors, mainframe computers and much more coming to the fore. The ideology of the US that had survived its rise into a colossus – that it was a free association of small-holding individuals, bound in a republic – came under immense pressure as a mass military–industrial consumer society invited people to find their happiness by being part of a vast single organisation. Political gnosticism was one way of preserving your independent citizenship apart from the state, by not being fooled, by knowing as much about it, as it did of you.

Political gnosticism's ever-expanding 'object' could accept all comers, including much that conventional left political discourse identified as actual conspiracy, like global banking funds and industry coordination groups such as the Trilateral Commission. From 1950s sci-fi through the 'paranoid style' of writers such as Thomas Pynchon, William Gaddis and Don DeLillo, to *The X-Files* and the *Matrix* movies, this gnostic empire would provide an enormous amount of material for popular culture. And it would become the permanent parallel world of the American imagination, after one day in Dallas in 1963 when President John F Kennedy – the hero of the 'new frontier' – was assassinated in plain view, certainly by Lee Harvey Oswald, very likely with the involvement of others. That was when the US and the world changed.

But even though a liberal prince had been killed, it would not be the left who took up the conspiracy. Instead, conspiracy and paranoia would become the default setting of the mainstream right.

This was something that the centre of the Republican Party had strived to avoid for a long time. They were, by the 1950s, a firmly right-wing party: pro-business, pro-American empire, no great champions of Black civil rights. But their main mission was to create an orderly politics that helped business to maximise growth and helped the global expansion of new transnational corporations, while maintaining a vigorous small-business sector, which would make communities reliably Republican – often through groups such as the Kiwanis or Shriners, which had become reliable booster organisations. President Eisenhower (Ike) – no leftist – had loathed Joe McCarthy, and didn't much like his lieutenant, congressman Richard Nixon, who became Eisenhower's VP, a demand of the party's centre-right. By the end of his second term, Ike had become wary of the fused sectors, which he named, in a parting speech, 'the military-industrial complex'. He and the moderates around him had fought a battle to keep the hard, anti-Communist right subordinate within the party, and the racist right out of it altogether.

But that all changed in the election of 1964. With the election of Kennedy's successor, Lyndon Johnson, assured as a vote to continue the JFK legacy, the Republican Party mainstream had little motivation to contest and the nomination was taken by the party's right faction candidate, Arizona senator Barry Goldwater. Fanatically pro-states' rights, opposed to the civil rights legislation that LBJ had brought in (urging global confrontation with the Soviets), Goldwater alienated many ordinary voters, and the Republicans went down to one of the greatest presidential losses of modern times, 61 per cent to 39 per cent. But the loss concealed a victory. The right had made their way back into the Republican Party and, for a while, held its centre. They would lose it again in 1968 to Richard Nixon – yes, Nixon was a centrist Republican – but by then they had put the paranoid style at the party's heart.

Johnson's victory in 1964 was the first and decisive announcement that the progressive social era was truly here.

The authority of white men, the church, the government, colleges, the army, was challenged. Both the Republican establishment and the wider white mainstream faced a clear challenge: accept that a whole new world was emerging and making demands for some of this freedom and equality, or retreat into a politics of fantasy, suspicion and paranoia. Spoiler alert.

The new politics of paranoid resentment couldn't have had a better representative than Richard Nixon, the son of Quakers from California, raised in a poverty and lovelessness he never stopped resenting. Prickly, raging, hypervigilant, an Iago become the Prince, he saw his ascension to the most powerful position in the world as, perhaps principally, a chance to destroy his enemies. Literal enemies. He had a list of them, running to the hundreds, and covering the liberal establishment in the media, academia and government. Nixon espoused centrist economic policies, but his inner sanctum was a reactionary clique, headed by his speechwriter Pat Buchanan. Buchanan was from a right-wing Catholic family, followers of Father Coughlin, an anti-Semitic preacher of the 1930s. He was what would later be described as a paleo-conservative – essentially those who believed that the US was really founded on a white ethnos and shared traditions, rather than the abstract sentiments of the founding documents. Following on from Buchanan came a collection of young Republicans, the most subsequently notorious being Roger Stone, whose devotion to Nixon was so great that he had his face tattooed on his back. Stone became a 'dirty hands' worker in the Committee to Re-Elect the President (CREEP) and was charged with sabotaging Democrat efforts to regain the White House at the 1972 presidential election.

With the country in uproar over Vietnam, the 1960s social revolution reaching its height, as was the widespread mainstream belief that the country had gone crazy. Nixon's invoking of a 'silent majority' – Buchanan's term – licensed the people who represented such, to do all they could to protect a society under attack. The result? Leaving nothing to 'chance' in the election, CREEP operatives had some Cuban anti-communist activists break into the office of the Democratic National Committee, housed in Washington DC's Watergate complex. Caught and arrested, one burglar had in his address book the phone number of Howard Hunt, an ex-CIA spy and now Nixon advisor.

From there, due to the investigative work of reporters Bob Woodward and Carl Bernstein, with a little help from anonymous tipoffs from the Associate Director of the FBI, Mark Felt (nicknamed 'Deep Throat') the conspiracy unravelled. It was revealed that Nixon had installed a secret taping system in the White House, to preserve every moment of what he expected to be a historic presidency. It was. In 1974, he became the first president to resign, ahead of impeachment and removal.

Over the next years the vast and paranoid scale of the Watergate conspiracy would be revealed. At the same time, in the Senate, a committee headed by Senator Frank Church was crawling all over the decades of the CIA's operations in fighting the Cold War, and exposing a vast and undemocratic scheme of global subversion. By the mid-1970s, the US government was revealed to be a vast stew of conspiracy, paranoia and secret apparatuses – all designed to protect a privilege whose demise was inevitable.

Such revelations made possible the election of Jimmy Carter, the first president in a long while to say that the US had to do things differently. His failure to do so made possible the victory of Ronald Reagan, and the first 'Make America Great Again' movement. Reagan's sunny disposition and optimism hid something dark behind the light: the paranoid and conspiratorial style was now at the centre of the right's politics. It would slumber and wake, but it would never be removed.

When the Democrats finally regained the White House in 1992, they did so with the first baby-boomer president, who had a generally liberal attitude to social policy, and a well-qualified wife as an extra. Everything about the Clintons stirred the deep recesses of conservatism to create what Hillary Clinton would later accurately call 'a vast right-wing conspiracy' against them, with hundreds of millions of dollars devoted to smearing their past, uncovering dark secrets and promoting perverse conspiracy. Bill Clinton sabotaged himself with his duplicitous exploitative affair with Monica Lewinsky, but the conspiracy would have continued anyway. Specialists in dark money (undisclosed political donations) such as billionaire Richard Mellon Scaife, started groups that accused the Clintons of having murdered their friend Vince Foster, of Hillary as being a secret lesbian witch and of protecting high-profile paedophiles and the like. It was in this stew of political conspiracy that the current conspiratorial style of the right was born, along with much of the raw material for Q. It would fall into abeyance, as the right gained actual power, and then roar back into life with the loss in the 2018 midterms, when it was clear they couldn't hold onto it.

## Cult decade: the 70s

Still, Nixon was right about one thing. In the 1970s, the US was going crazy. Much of the optimism had run out of the social revolution, and that decade became the time of the cult, the fad and the crazy tale. What had started with the Mormons' mad story of the world had now flowered in every direction. Everyone had a story to tell, the crazier the better.

Young tourists doing the 'hippie trail' – the now unimaginable trek from Europe, through Afghanistan, Iran and Kashmir, to East Asia – came into contact with Eastern religions and found in their world-spirit an alternative to the narrower focus and political conservatism of Western monotheism. These religions followed them back to the West: Bhaktivedanta Swami Prabhupada founded the first Hare Krishna information centre in New York in 1965, moving to San Francisco in 1966. Hare Krishna offered a simplified version of complex Hindu mysticism and worldview to a West that Hindu divines saw as spiritually bereft. Eastern religion had been coming across to Europe for 150 years by then, with many high-profile followers and gurus, and a few people peeling off into communes and closed communities. The Hare Krishna were different. Here for the first time was a religious cult, in the centre of cities, persuading thousands of young people to leave their families and friends, change their names and work in an ever-expanding network in the pursuit of enlightenment and a state of being qualitatively different from what many saw as the cramped and anxious life of the West.

Prabhupada's move to San Francisco was a wild success. The 'summer of love' of 1967 carried the Hare Krishna message far and wide, and in the 1970s cults simply became part of the landscape of everyday life.

The Unification Church appeared – followers of the Korean Reverend Sun Myung Moon – and rapidly became ubiquitous, Reverend Moon's young roboticised devotees selling flowers at airports, and working 100-hour weeks to fund the Church's vast expansion. The 'Moonies', as they were known, specialised in recruitment by 'love bombing'. This involved finding lonely young people in big cities – often backpackers for whom the great adventure had become one of loss and separation – and giving them intensely positive engagement, often for days or weeks at a time. Those they managed to draw in were then put to work. Reverend Moon moved to the US in 1971, and focused his energy on the Church there. The Moonies' most distinctive practice was the mass wedding, in which thousands of couples were wed in arranged marriages in stadiums, rented by Moon himself, standing on a huge podium. By this time, frantic parents were hiring private detectives to kidnap their children and hold them for days while psychologically trained 'deprogrammers' tried to counteract their indoctrination.

But the Krishnas and the Moonies were just two among many cults that catered to every social strata and need. Shopfront churches and numerous street churches of Jesus sprang up in poorer cities; self-help and shaping movements such as Synanon and EST sprang up among the Hollywood glitterati. Scientology, a minority movement from the 1940s, became massively popular, offering adherents the chance to 'clear' their mind of 'engrams' – traumatic unconscious memories creating neuroses. Within Christianity, the traditional churches were yielding followers to the new evangelism – spectacular revival meetings deriving from pentecostalist and dispensationalist teachings, taking place in dedicated megachurches and televised through their own TV shows and, eventually, whole networks.

Within the 1970s, such cults were only a part of the story. For a rising generation of boomers, and for the children who would become Generation X, thousands of fads and fashions were now being offered that would achieve, at an individual level, the transcendence that the 60s had offered through collective revolution. This included biorhythms, crystals, encounter groups, group therapy, cognitive behavioural therapy, primal screaming, neurolinguistic programming, Rolfing, sensory deprivation tanks, transformative diets – the Scarsdale, the Atkins, the Pritikin, the Israeli Army, the grapefruit – and a vast enthusiasm for esoteric knowledge that had hitherto been confined to dusty occult bookshops: the true origin of the pyramids, visits by aliens, cow abductions, anal probes, the Bermuda Triangle, spoon-bending telekinesis, the works.

The end of this fast-flying carousel of new possibilities can be reasonably precisely dated to 19 November 1978, when troops from the army of the South American country of Guyana, together with news crews, reached the collective farm-commune of the Peoples Temple, Jonestown. There, they found the bodies of more than 900 men, women and children, lying dead around the vats of the soon-to-be-notorious 'Kool Aid' (it was actually Flavor Aid, a cheaper variant), laced with cyanide that had been the means of their mass suicide and murder. Founded and led by the charismatic Reverend Jim Jones in Indianapolis in 1955, the Peoples Temple Full Gospel Church attracted a large following.

Under increasing pressure from US tax authorities, and his own pill-fuelled paranoia, Jones decamped in 1977 with the core faithful to a large community in a harsh zone near the equator. Worried relatives had started a campaign to have Jonestown investigated; when a congressman and news crew flew south to investigate, they were greeted with a Potemkin display of happy children dancing, but were also petitioned by people wishing to leave. The visitors were ambushed at the airport and killed. Knowing that the authorities would come for them, Jones and his four faithful female lieutenants/concubines put the final plan into action.

There would be other cults to come after Jonestown. The most spectacular was the Rajneesh movement, the Orange People, led by Bhagwan Shree Rajneesh, who offered a Hare Krishna variant, amassing a huge following in the US with the same model as others: ceaseless work, the sexual availability of female followers to the leader under a 'free love' rubric, vast wealth, the flaunting of said wealth by the ascetic leader – Bhagwan owned dozens of Rolls-Royces – and large real estate holdings. The Rajneeshees would eventually own a chunk of Oregon, and attempt to take over local town councils with assassinations and restaurant poisonings, which caused them to be broken up by mass prosecution in 1985.

But this was very much a late farcical version of the earlier tragedy.[29] By the time 'Jonestown' hit the news, the whole 60s and 70s period had already been running out of steam – a product of its furious and diminishing need for novelty, transgression and edge. This event pretty much killed its remaining fantasies stone dead. Particularly shocking perhaps was the rendering of the death scene, in the cheap colour of TV video – bodies piled on bodies, in the slacks and sundresses of the era. It was a shattering repudiation of the decade's operating premise: that all these whacky things were, if not a path to transcendence, then a welcome bit of necessary exploration, and if nothing else, some fun. The strong sweet lime cordial drink in the vats at Jonestown, used to blunt the bitterness of cyanide, especially for the children, gave a phrase to the era that would follow. The followers of Jim Jones had 'drunk the Kool-Aid'.

## Progress to progressivism

The 1970s were a transitional period between two cultural eras. The moral order that had held until the 60s – one of institutional authority, conventional and abstemious behaviour – had finally collapsed, leaving the pursuit of desire as the dominant organising principle. The new order, the one we live in, where surveillance replaces value-internalisation, social moralising replaces authority and governments rule by reshaping behaviour, was not yet here. In the interim was the decade or so when everything could happen.

When that new order did take over, it was the left – as the embodiment of progressivism – that became dominant, with lawyers, educationalists and others reshaping social life; and censorious progressivism on matters of race, gender etc., replacing the libertinism of the sexual revolution. As we have seen, the further rise of this new group and its social imperatives gave Donald Trump a prime target for his campaign. Progressivism, in our era, arises when the knowledge and information economy become dominant; society produces a trained social class to run it, and that new class's necessarily universalist and critical ways of thinking predispose them to question old and inherited values. When you have millions of such people whose job is to question given processes and ways of doing things, their values are going to be that it is good to question given things and that everything should be as rational and equal as possible. Not only does anti-racism and anti-sexism become imperative, but opinions or thought behaviours that are racist or sexist, or simply traditional as regards certain preferences, come to be seen as abhorrent.

Since those people holding such opinions are often from the older, manual working class or small business class, who have been largely locked out of the information/knowledge revolution, such a culture war is really a class war. With the left – the progressives – taking the role of 'superego', the conscience, the denier of pleasure (the very opposite of its role in the 60s and 70s), the right becomes the agency of pleasure, desire and anarchy. This process was on steroids by 2010 and served as the prelude to Trump – joyous ressentiment's Frankenstein monster loosed on the world. Could this obsessive insistence that a morality must be imposed be sufficient to characterise twenty-first century progressivism as a cult?

### Drag Queen Storytime in the shadow of the monument
*Washington DC, Adams Morgan neighbourhood, November 2022.*

There was a big bearded bloke in a canary yellow tracksuit clambering all over the modernisty big block man statue when I arrived at Unity Park for Drag Queen Storytime. The park is a small green triangle in front of the classical portico of the public library, surrounded by cafes, both hip and old skool. This is Adams Morgan, an area to the north of Washington DC proper. It's a jumble of row houses and a couple of lively shopping streets, and known as the 'last funky neighbourhood in DC'.

The statue was one of those post-war 'soaring humanity' type things, a blocky humanoid figure with a blocky humanoid child on its shoulders. It's five minutes until the showtime listed on the neighbourhood's groovy website, drag queen reader Venus Valhalla sits to one side in scarlet and pink, putting the final touches to her makeup, as a chunky double-denimed assistant set up the mike and amplifier. Canary man was still holding on to the statue like King Kong. Was he part of this? A local maddie? As he started to clamber down, a stream of tiny rainbows filled the bright air. A bubble machine! He was setting up a bubble machine.

Valhalla's assistant put out some brightly coloured mats, a big pile of picture books arrived from the library and Miss Venus seated herself in the comfy chair. And waited. And waited some more. Couples, mostly white, with small kids streamed this way and that; party boys (mostly Black), still in their sexy Halloween S&M wings. The leaves stirred, the bubbles blew. Oh dear. What if they gave a drag queen story hour and nobody came?

This was the Sunday morning after Halloween Saturday night and the weather had turned, there was a real chill in the air. I'd arrived late, not knowing what to expect from Drag Queen Storytime, new cockpit of the culture wars, but was at least expecting an audience. The sole protester was an old heavyset Hispanic woman on the other side of the road, hanging a banner about the miracle of Fatima. Eventually, one white trio turned up, then another: single-child families, the men hipster-schlubby, the women all knitwear and long dark hair, like NPR presenters. Soon there were about six groups and Miss Venus began: 'This is called *Glitter Everywhere!*'

Of course it was. Most of the kids were paying no attention at all, just playing on the mats. Across the road Fatima lady couldn't hear a thing, but crossed herself anyway. A couple of older Hispanic guys walked past, chatting, then going silent as they saw Miss Venus, like a giant red velvet cupcake, then scowled and moved on.

Errol wasn't so sure. He's been a local for some decades, he looked thirty but could have been ninety. He stood at the edge of the park, a beige corduroy cap in hand, shifting from one leg to the other. 'This is messed up,' he said, as loudly as he could without shouting. 'This is really messed up!'

'Time for another story,' Miss Venus intoned. With the very young crowd, the assistant brought out a board book about the size of a folding card table. 'Would you tell a flamingo she couldn't be pink?' a cartoon pig said in Venus-inflected tones. The final act was a book called *Neither*, in which a blob is neither one colour nor the other and eventually goes to the Land of They. A dozen pairs of eyes shone, brimming with wonder, as they stared up at the funny lady. They belonged to the NPR parents. The kids just weren't into it.

As far as culture war skirmishes go, it was something of a fizzer.

During the middle parts of the journey to the Land of They, I'd sidled up to canary tracksuit man, whose name was Brian and was running the gig for the Adams Morgan Business Development Outfit. 'We organised these with the public library.' They'd been running for six months. He couldn't honestly remember who had decided on a drag queen story hour for the time and space. 'To teach kids about diversity and acceptance. The community supports it.'

'Come on,' I said, a little angry now, 'I saw half a dozen people walk by, all either Black or Hispanic, and they make it clear they really didn't. That's the same number here.'

'No, the community supports it.' One's suspicion was that a working-class and artistic neighbourhood of colour – one-time home of James Baldwin and Gil Scott-Heron – was being culturally transformed for a progressive population.

'I have to go, check our website.' He dived in energetically to pick up mats. Venus had already departed, having changed her 70s clog heels for flats and made a break for the bus.

So, yes, it was a little pathetic on both sides. But this was culture war, American style, no mistake about it. You want story time with a bit of colour and movement to take your kids to? It's going to be Drag Queen Storytime or nothing, and the kicker story will be how much cooler it is to be neither this nor that. Australians, Brits: we can't do the full culture war, some sense of the absurd always gets to us. Americans: they witness, they preach, the virtuous heart is abroad in the world, shining like a rainbow bubble.

**The cult of progressivism**

This is principally a book about the cult lines that flowed into the contemporary American right. In writing it, I've made attempts to distinguish a rational right tradition from the conspiratorial-cult version, and show how the latter has gradually taken over the former. Nothing new there, but the question of whether it is determined by the very nature of the American entity is not often asked. So it's also worth asking the question: has the American left, or parts of it, travelled in the same direction, and to the same degree? The answer to the second part is a very obvious 'no'. What is usually known as the 'centre-left' (and which many leftists would see as the centre, or centre-right) is, in our era, the dominant form of state rationality. A thumbnail description would be that it is a form of moderate neoliberal governance, with social market and minor social democratic features, and a 'progressive' social-cultural form. Its leaders and commanders are overwhelmingly trained in a virtual identical form of statecraft the world over: politics consists of managing a neoliberal, substantially private economy, supplementing that with a very limited state, doing only what the market cannot do; and generally letting the culture change in a direction determined by media and social flows, which is 'progressive'.

What do we mean by 'progressive'? When the Progressive Party was an engine of change in America in the early twentieth century, 'progressive' related primarily to economic matters – the creation of a large public sector, higher wages, union rights, planned cities, etc. – with full equality for Black people, and some change in women's rights and roles. But such progressivism assumed that the social and cultural form of life was substantially fixed: the family was the unit of society, women did most of the nurturing, racial communities were largely self-contained and a nation tended to be ethnically dominated by one group. Since right and left both agreed on these matters – very few questioned them, so there was no act of agreement needed – politics was near wholly concerned with how the economy and state were organised. As we have seen, new social groups organised around education and knowledge were responsible for the distinctive character of the social revolution of the 1960s. As the knowledge society expanded, these groups became something of a class in their own right, and their increasing power from the 1990s onwards began to determine the overall form of the culture.

In the 2010s, late millennials and Gen Z – anyone who had been raised in the smartphone/social media/diversity web – burst onto the scene of teenage and adult life, and society was subject to culture wars every bit as dramatic as had been seen in the 1960s. But now, it was not the bohemian values of a small cultural group spreading out to mass culture. It was the core social values of the 30 per cent or so of people whose lives had been formed within the new 'knowledge economy' culture, and, as we have seen, they were driving it with all the force of their massive social power.

This was the era in which the very microprocesses of social life began to be examined and consciously reconstructed. Sexist and racist texts from the past required 'trigger warnings' for students who might be traumatised by encountering them. Moments that might have been seen as mildly gauche or neutral, such as asking where someone was from, came to be characterised as 'microaggressions'. The older notion of 'structural racism' expanded into the idea of 'whiteness', a far more encompassing cultural notion of oppression.

Within this onslaught on inherited cultural oppression, there was a heroic narrative too. The working-class man as revolutionary hero had been replaced by women, non-whites and gays and lesbians. As these groups gained substantial equality, this was followed by the stateless refugee and then by the trans person. These were genuinely heroic. But with this heroic narrative came an adamantine certainty, collectively exercised, in the truth of a particular vision of social life.

Paradoxically, the particularity of this vision was that everything must be universal and generalised, in moral terms, and that there was no legitimacy to the other, the conservative side of the argument – such as the case for preserving marriage as between a man and a woman, anchored by fertility.

The wave of cultural action that followed came from progressives who saw the new morality as demanding the limiting of circulation of books and screen media with racist, sexist or otherwise offensive themes and terms – everything from *Huckleberry Finn* to *Friends* – and a shutting-down of debate about the nature of sex and gender, of the extent to which racism through slavery was not merely essential to American history, but the totality of its origins, as appeared to be claimed by the *New York Times'* 1619 Project.[30] The notion that the other side should not even be heard – because the impact of such words would be materially damaging – put 'identity' at the centre of life in ways no other culture did. And it seems clear that the strength of such a movement came in part from its drawing on notions of the 'pursuit of happiness', lying at the core of the very formation of the state and its sovereignty – and hence the subjectivity of its people. In this sense, it seems reasonable to say that such a movement has become a cult, looking to a single principle of good to answer the moral and existential questions of a messy, multiple world.

### Ride the tiger

This period of American history can also be read in another way, in terms of the old saying that 'a paranoic is someone in possession of the facts'. It is easy enough to say that American working-class people were subject to the great tides of history in the loss of their prestige and power. But it's also clear that they were subject to a conspiracy in which the post–Cold War elite – at the nexus of politics, business and academia, and oriented to a universal neoliberalism – had agreed among themselves that Western economies would have to be globalised, that this would result in the destruction of the West's industrial base and its dependent working class, and that this would have to be lied about for several years until the process was too advanced to be reversed. This is the story of the WTO, the GATT and the North American Free Trade Agreement.

Equally, there's no doubt that the path to war following 9/11 had been plotted in the 1990s, when neoconservatives on both the left and right of US politics conceived the 'project for a new American century' (PFANAC), which argued that by projecting its power globally with overwhelming force, the US could hold off the demographic rise of China and India and the resultant tilt of the world eastward. Several of the main players in the PFANAC, such as Paul Wolfowitz, had been students of the enigmatic magus, Leo Strauss, a political philosopher at the University of Chicago. Strauss (who died in 1973) taught a Platonic-derived notion that contemporary societies should be steered by a self-knowing elite, steeped in European philosophy and culture, and with a pessimistic view of the human condition. In the US, the role of these guardians was to counterbalance the naive optimism and human perfectionism that sprang from US culture and was reproduced by its constitutional order, with a guiding hand that presumed humanity to be irreparably brutal, irrational, self-defeating and destructive. The US pursued mastery in this dark picture, simply to stay alive. Strauss was a lifelong correspondent with

Carl Schmitt, the Nazi-aligned political philosopher who developed the idea that all modern, democratic states rely for their order on the rule of 'exception', whereby the preservation of the public order must be guaranteed by the very act – dictatorship, audacity, sudden violence – that the society purports to explicitly exclude.

These shadowy movements of an intellectual-political elite are not discussed in detail here because this is largely a story about how the currents of American culture and politics have intersected among the masses. But it would be an error to forget them, in considering how the US and the world got to where it is now, even if other accounts tend to exaggerate their importance. Conspiracies such as those which created the Iraq War are also relatively rational and self-knowing, even if they eventually fall into delusion of a less exotic kind. In the Trump era, one might say that mass cultishness and elite conspiracy came together in the person of Steve Bannon – a follower of the darkest tradition on the right, the political occultism of Julius Evola and others. Evola, a reactionary philosopher of the early twentieth century who considered Mussolini to be hopelessly moderate, saw modernity as a great pestilence, one that would eventually consume itself, at which point an elite would restore a world of traditional values: the celebration of war, masculinity and conquest, and the triumphant masterful ego. Until then, Evola argued, such conspirators must 'ride the tiger' – that is, get along with modernity, without falling off and getting consumed by it. All very much in control until someone loses an 'I'.

The problem with having an elite conspiracy (ride the tiger) that's as nuts as the mass conspiracy (the QAnon cult), is that you can't actually steer, or govern, anything because each conspiracy threatens to tear the other apart. Elite conspiracies only work when they are rational as to ends and means, accepting the world as it is, to be manipulated. Without such, the Trump team had the dilemma that their movement was being drawn by the whackiest parts of the QAnon cult. And the QAnon cult was, as we have seen, probably two guys making stuff up on the 8chan chatboard.

How had it come to this for the republic that was the last, best hope of man? Is it possible that in its end was its beginning?

# 6.
# THE FOUNDING

Remember the Boston Tea Party? Of course, you do! Like many Australians, you either got a burst of American history somewhere in school – quite possibly more than you got on Australian history – or you've picked it up through a hundred stray movies and mentions. Something about destroying tea in the harbour, people dressed as American Indians, then someone wrote a declaration and then independence. Tax, yes. Taxation without representation!

The American Revolution is presented as the supreme product of the Enlightenment, or one branch of it anyway; the moment when decades of debate about free thought and the rights of man took material form, as citizens of the American colonies rose up in violent insurrection against the hideous imposition of a … stamp tax. The truth is, the more you question it, the more your secure knowledge of the founding of the US starts to come apart. Was it really about the sale of tea? Surely there's more to it than that?

There is. More to it, and also less. The 'American Revolution' and the subsequent war for independence were two events that were really multiple overlapping events that coalesce in the historical memory.

### Sons and daughters of liberty

Right from their founding in the 1600s, the American colonies, especially Massachusetts, had enjoyed a different relationship between civil order, ideas, books and rank. Founded by religious seekers after truth, their societies had none of the English assumptions of aristocracy and fixity of that role. By the late 1600s, they had colleges, publishers and intense debate. In the 1700s, as their maritime cities grew, they felt themselves to be heirs to the Glorious Revolution of 1688 in which, after a century of struggle, Anglicans, aristocrats and the rising town burghers had managed to stabilise a basic set of rights and a constitutional monarchy. But in this very stability lay its undoing. By the 1760s, George III and his court had overridden Britain's revolutionary self-conception to wage wars in Europe and began to see the colonies as a potential cash cow. The new taxes may have annoyed many in the US merchant cities, but the majority of those people never imagined for a moment that such grievances were sufficient cause for rebellion. But for Samuel Adams, James Otis, and other college-educated men, it was an opportunity to make a new revolution, with a 'strategy of tension'.

By 1768, garrisoned troops were policing Boston. Samuel Adams then used a combination of agitation and political theatre, including a macabre funeral procession, to turn a lethal encounter into the Boston Massacre of 1770. By 1775 the radicals had the open conflict they had wanted, supercharged by the sensational 1776 Boston publication of Thomas Paine's *Common Sense*. This suggestion that independence was the natural state was reinforced by the Declaration of Independence, largely drafted by the radical philosopher, plantation- (and slave-) owner, anti-Christian Deist, Thomas Jefferson. The Declaration's radical wording gave the rebellion a world historical character, and no route back. If the rebels lost, the British state would impose direct rule on its colonies, and humanity would take a step backwards.

When victory was achieved in 1781, and Great Britain recognised the USA in 1783, the revolutionaries saw the hand of God and providence in the result. In its initial form, the USA was the most radically free society in the world – for those who were free (for the slaves it was a disaster).[31] But the 'loose' version of the United States lasted a mere four years. By 1787, it was clear that this loose confederation of free states was a sitting duck for European imperial powers and disgruntled groups from within, and so a new Constitution was voted up, enshrining a president as leader. This elected monarch was less powerful than European kings, but over centuries as monarchs have been replaced by prime ministers, the president has gained semi-divine status: a man with the right – by American view anyway – to use nuclear weapons on America's enemies, real or imagined.

In 1803, President Thomas Jefferson, whose initial vision of the country had been semi-anarchist, purchased from France the vast Louisiana Territory, stretching from the Gulf of Mexico to Canada. He didn't ask Congress to pass a law to do it, he just did it. And thus set a precedent for presidential action. In 1823, President James Monroe would issue what became known as the Monroe Doctrine – warning off interference from European powers in the affairs of the Western Hemisphere; and President Andrew 'Bloody' Jackson would open the West by driving Native Americans off their lands – a genocidal process that even many of his contemporaries found appalling. And so it went. The US became a society more embodied in one man, more shaped by his personality and projection of such, than France under Louis XIV, the Sun King.

### The Constitution-machine

When the Constitution was drafted and the first ten amendments – the Bill of Rights – immediately added, the framers conceived of the Supreme Court as the least of the three separated powers. Congress made laws, the president executed them, and the Court ruled on matters concerning inter-state actors or clashes in states' laws. But in 1803, the Court brought down the ruling in *Marbury v Madison*, concerning matters of government appointments. In making its judgement, the Court came to the conclusion that the Constitution as written only made sense if the Court could rule laws and executive actions as 'unconstitutional' and prevent them from being applied.

With one leap, the Supreme Court had become one of the most powerful, and certainly one of the strangest, institutions in this or any land. Purporting to find reason in justice, Supreme Court judges work either by finding the spirit in the Constitution (the liberals) or its literal intent (the conservatives). It has endorsed state racism (in 1897), then declared it illegal (in 1954), found abortion to be a right, then said such was an absurdity.

Actually, for much of its history, the Supreme Court didn't interfere with laws that were plainly unconstitutional, such as those censoring a host of radical political material, or state laws enforcing religion. But in 1962, the *Engel v Vitale* case banned prayer in public (state) schools in the US. This enforced the First Amendment's ban on established religion; but it also cut across the profoundly Christian nature of everyday American life. From *Engel* onwards, evangelical Christians got interested in politics, as the abstract constitutional system created one liberal right after another in a conservative social order. Conservatives saw laws protecting pornography and abortion as abominations created *ab nihilo* as an act of secular faith. In the 2000s, the conservatives finally gained control and, among many other things, removed all protections for African-American voters, and granted the right to spend unlimited money on political slush funds. The sense, on each dissenting side, was of a machine cranking out new laws. This is an expression of the Constitution's rationalistic character, embodying the mechanistic mind of the Anglo-American side of the Enlightenment.

Thus the Constitution and its distributive mechanisms became an agency for the very thing they had hoped to prevent: an extremism formed around notions of simple and unique truths, to be imposed on others. By the 1990s, the politics of the US were split between cultural and economic imperatives. By the 2010s, culture was perhaps the dominant organising power within politics. Millions of those on the Republican side believed themselves to be insurgents against a liberal 'system', on behalf of a traditional 'lifeworld', and Christian evangelism and Pentecostalism were the very kernel of it. The cult of the US had produced cults who saw the very founding abstract principles of the country as a betrayal of its concrete and real spirit. It was this adhering to the concrete, the mythical, the non-abstract, the anti-systemic, the veiled and the occult that would serve as the prelude to the Trump triumph and the rise of QAnon.

What could be more stark an example of this than the Supreme Court's handling of the issue of guns, and the creation of a republic of mayhem, out of the Second Amendment's commitment to the right to bear arms? The conservatives feed the machine by asking how muskets were distributed in an agrarian eighteenth century, and six months later survivalists sell assault rifles to disturbed young men at gun shows. The US has five times the murders of comparable societies and a hecatomb of children dead from accidents.[32] Those who say 'it's not just the guns' are right; it's the clash of an atomised and anomic country with plentiful firearms, and the chance to blast your way through the society that spurns you.

Gun violence is a major contributor to the perverse anti-modern fatalism that pervades the most technologically advanced market society in the world; the beggars' consolation is that whatever happens was somehow meant to. Over the decades, this has undermined the country's capacity to recognise nemesis – the adversarial force against all life. This has been manifested in the anonymous massacre: first, snipers from clocktowers, then in postal service offices, then in McDonald's and finally in schools. After Uvalde in 2022, when police lingered for an hour while seven-year-olds texted for help before being slaughtered, the machine and its sick seance with the mind of the founders should have come to an end.

For these organisations – the NRA, the Heritage Foundation, the Supreme Court – Uvalde should have been a moment of exception; when individuals step back from an ideology or rigid belief and, in the name of the basic principles of life itself, say that a false path has been taken, that something must change. That didn't happen. And because it didn't, something in America died. Many Americans felt it; as did many of its observers, including this writer. It seemed that what had died within America, was America itself. What sources of renewal remain?

# CONCLUSION
## AMERICAN REASON

*Louisville, Kentucky, 6 November 2022, two days before the midterm elections.*

Westminster Avenue in a bougie suburb of Louisville – faux colonial houses, white porches and coach lamps, late afternoon light streaming through orange leaves. Four of us from the 'Protect Kentucky [Abortion] Access' canvassing group SE8 are straggling across lawns and sidewalks and at the tenth house we hit, it appeared as if Diana, our veteran member (80+, short-cut white hair and Japanese print slacks), was going to kidnap a dog. It was a tiny hairy thing and it had come flying out to greet us, ahead of its owner, a large woman lumbering out from the garage behind.

'Come on boy, come on little feller,' Diana had said, as it had leapt into her arms.

'Is this about politics?' said the woman, rolling forward in grey sweatpants and blue sweat top. 'I don't wanna talk about no politics.'

## CONCLUSION

'Let's move on to th–,' said Alli, canvassing co-ordinator, checking a house list on her phone. This is the standard procedure of these things – it's a get-out-the-vote drive, not a mobile debating society. The danger of actually arguing with someone is that you'll get the other side's vote out, through sheer orneriness.

Diana hadn't got that memo. Or if she had, she'd ignored it. She let the dog go, but it stayed round her, licking her fingers. 'I just wanted to say a couple of things to you. The first is that amendment two would put the lives of thousands of Kentuckian women in danger …'

'Come here, Marmalade,' the woman said, not able to walk away without her dog. She might have glanced nervously over at Diana's battered car we'd arrived in, which had bumper stickers going back to the Iraq War on the back. Was this blackmail?

'The other thing I want to say,' Diana continued, 'yesssssss, gooooooood boy – is that they've put a weasel phrase about banning public funds for abortion. Well there's no provision for state public funds, there never has been, it's a complete deception … go on, boy.' Diana shooed the dog off.

'Well yes I'll think about it …' said the woman, pushing the dog inside with her toe. Diana rejoined us. Was Alli about to say something? It wouldn't have mattered. The smile on Diana's face said it all. Argument made. Damn the rest. Quite possibly it's a vote for the other side, but who the hell knows?

Who the hell knows anything about how politics works anymore? Here we were, out in the suburban nowhere of Louisville, a mid-size Midwest city of a million and a half people, traipsing around to find six to a dozen votes if we're lucky, to stop an anti-abortion 'ballot measure', one of the umpteen referendum questions put on US ballots each election. Amendment Two is a pre-emptive strike. Its core clause asks you to affirm that: 'To protect human life, nothing in this Constitution shall be construed to secure or protect a right to abortion or require the funding of abortion.'

In other words, the Kentucky Supreme Court couldn't find the same implicit right to privacy that the US Supreme Court found in the US Constitution via *Roe v Wade*. It's one of a number of such measures being offered in the wake of the Supreme Court Dobbs decision, overturning Roe. But it's of importance beyond others because it's a test as to whether total abortion bans can be defeated in solid Republican states. In the primary season in Kansas, a few months earlier, an early-run abortion ban measure had been roundly defeated, and they don't get much more red-state than Kansas. It was a huge boost to the idea that the conservative vote could be split on this issue, mainly along gender lines. In the privacy of the ballot box, certain raw facts of life assert themselves.

So Kentucky is now the test of whether the Kansas win was a one-off or a more sustained and promising political division. Possibly a one-off, because the right were complacent and unprepared, so soon after Dobbs, and the left made it an imperative: win or lose, they were going to show there was resistance. Whether they would have won without the element of surprise is a hypothetical question, but you only get that kind of luck once. The right have got their forces out everywhere, in a half dozen different groups named on the 'Yes/2' conjunction in various combinations, and they've also modified their message. Now they're targeting Joe Biden's announcement that he would pursue the legal codification of a right to legal abortion, if he had control of Congress. The suggestion is that this would legalise abortion on demand to term. It wouldn't, even though a minority are arguing for that. But it would have a necessary provision for 'life of the mother' abortion to term. In a polity where Republicans are even arguing against 'life of the mother' abortions, that's enough for the right to make campaigns around. On these matters, hardcore progressives can underestimate just how provisional many people's support for legal abortion is. You'll be shocked to hear that American progressives can be a little blithe sometimes.

We got a great example of that when our three teams of two met up at the canvassing focus, at a Starbucks in a mid-size mall nearby. I latched onto one team – short-haired, sensible shorts types – to ask a few questions; it got rough immediately. 'We work together, we're physicians. Yes, I'm a Democrat. Why are you asking all these questions?'

'Well erggh journalist me, come a long way, big plane,' I sort of burbled. 'This is a key political issue.'

'It's not a political issue,' one pretty much snapped. 'It's a medical issue, a –'

'Well, yeah,' I said, adopting the grinning Aussie doofus pose, 'but if the other side says it's political, then you've got a fight'.

As with all American canvassing, canvassing everywhere I guess, it was going to be a matter of a couple of short hops between areas identified as maximally disposed to vote 'No', and minimally likely to be riled to vote 'Yes'.

Now, we were all looking at a car with a cut-out of Ruth Bader Ginsburg stuck to the side back window – 'when you ride, you ride with RBG' – and trying to work out which house it belonged to.

'Well, we moved into a retirement home seven years ago, my husband and I,' Diana had said on the drive over. 'And that gave me more time for activism. I mean you know I voted Republican for a long time, but I really didn't like it when … Shoot, you know …'

'Bush,' I said.

'No, earlier.'

'Reagan?' said Alli, twenty-seven, dredging high school memory.

'No, Watergate … Nixon!'

'Wow,' Alli and I both said involuntarily.

'It was Bush, Bush II, I really got involved over, when I became a pastor.'

'A pastor?'

'In the United Church of Christ, and then you couldn't stop me.'

Nixon, puritan pastors, Dubya. We were on a lawn with raked, fiery leaves, plastic glowing Halloween skulls pinned around its edges and squirrels cavorting round the trees. Americana overload.

'When was your first campaign, Diana?'

'Oh, that would have been St Louis, in 1964, for handicapped spaces for the hospital parking lot.'

'Then civil rights …'

'Yes! My church was going to have Martin Luther King speak, but …'

'What happened?'

She looked at me. We moved on.

'Not this house,' said Alli.

'But it's got a squirrel crossing,' I said. Someone had painted a sort of pedestrian crossing over the driveway serving four houses and put up a stop sign.

Could that be? People looking out for squirrels, but not necessarily opposed to a total ban on abortion? The answer is yes.

The most startling development of the anti-abortion 'pro-life' movement has been the removal of the 'life of the mother' exception. The 'incest and rape' exception went a while ago, on the grounds that if you believe the embryo/foetus to be a person with full rights, then why should it pay for the sins of others? The 'life of the mother' exception started to be eroded in Republican primaries as candidates made a bid for the votes of the religious right, and was then rolled over into general campaigns. Then, in the era of COVID and 'fake news', Republicans began asserting that there was no need for a 'life of the mother' exception because medical science had made every such complication curable. It's a line you hear more and more, the new orthodoxy; it's especially absurd given that the US has childbirth death rates far higher than the rest of the West, and for some groups such as Black women, developing nation levels.

For ever larger parts of the anti-abortion movement, 'life' has become this quality so abstracted and alienated from the people doing the actual living that it is prior to any actual manifestation of it. The demand for 'life' as a sort of ultimate ground comes from a society that is breaking itself apart with a predatory capitalism, and a technology-driven culture that turns every aspect of existence, for many millions, into a struggle to actually live. The less life is offered to actual people, as an aspect of their personhood, the more the abstract entity of 'life' becomes elevated as a transcendental value.[33]

People like Diana, who will not accept it, save the place. She was a walking half-century of protest, an example of the country's better half, and not above giving someone the slight sense she might hold their dog till they agreed to vote 'No to 2'. As I left, traipsing through the streets of colonialalia, with yard signs for Congress, judge, water services supervisor staked into lawns, Diana was making a baby-toting man, who was going to vote, commit to vote. 'Yes ma'am, I will.' More power to her, and to all who believe that politics is the movement of the spirit, the persuasion to justice, as, in the dark, the coach lamps came on.

### Take it on the run, baby

Louisville was like dozens I'd encountered in fifteen years of traipsing around the US: one storied in legend, baseball, Louis Armstrong and jazz, Hunter Thompson, civil rights and much more. But the streets of shops and row houses, the civic buildings and squares, the train station and streetcars were beyond gone; replaced with an arid centre of block-size carparks, megahotels and conference centres, plus a few plaques where life had once flourished. The old city had been swept away like hundreds of other cities in the 1970s and 80s; after Black people had moved in and risen up against the systemic racism, and white people had left, and the centre had been planed flat and sold off as lots.

What America did to its cities and towns in that period is something it has never really recovered from, because there is no actual politics without a *polis*. What the country got instead was vast rings of suburbs with malls connected by

CONCLUSION

freeways. Now the malls are dying and all that's left are the strips of fast food joints along the freeways. For fifteen years, since I'd first hit this extraordinary post-civilisation for the 2008 elections, I'd endured the growing horror at what the US had done to what was formerly a global fund of twentieth-century culture, by revelling in the postmodern, Baudrillardian simulacrum of it all.

This trip, for the 2022 midterms, was the last I could possibly make in that spirit. There was nothing left to see except what was being left out. For the first time in this gig, I had started to think about the air miles and the emissions I was generating for what might be a single story that went nowhere. Right at the start I had determined that a centrepiece of the coverage would be a trip to Texas to see, at Smoky's Bar n Grill in Fort Worth, REO Speedwagon, the venerable stadium rock band, extant since 1967, but who had had a string of hits in the early 80s, coinciding with my early adolescence. Their bright sound and fizzy guitar had seemed like the promise not only that music makes to the young – a three-minute utopia expressing or accompanying the ecstasy and agony of sex and desire – but the promise America made to the outlying colonies of its culture, of an impossibly shiny and exciting otherworld that would lift everyone out of the dull suburbanism of an Australian childhood.

It turned out that it was America that was the drear reality. Forty years after 'Keep on Lovin' You' had echoed from boomboxes in the warm night, bright lights shimmering on the pool and beachside, REO were still speedwagoning around the country, playing whatever gigs they could get. The story would write itself – the Texas sprawl, the boomer-gen X crowd, the buffalo wings, the band still in its

80s lineup opening one of those musical wormholes to your youth.

I couldn't do it. This year, contemplating the sheer level of burn coming out of the back of the plane, it felt like some sort of other great divide had come down. This world of American plenty, the surplus and abundance of mass culture, which quite possibly proved more beguiling to Australians than it proved to Americans themselves, this all seemed part of a past world, there with the 70s with biorhythms and dolphins and pet rocks and Fleetwod Mac's *Rumours* and bad sitcoms, and the distant promise and possibility of Los Angeles or New York – the discursive field of dreams in which many of us had lived for decades. But in dreams begin responsibility, and now here it was, a bounded world whose way of being in we are going to have to change, and pretty fast.

Instead, I was in Louisville. And of course in its quiet way it was the story of the election, the one progressivism, the rational side of it, would 'win', relatively speaking. It was worth going there, as it is always worth going somewhere, to feel a living continuity with the best of American resistance, its plain courage and refusal to yield, and how, passed from man to woman, from hand to hand, the dream lives on.

### She stoops to conk out?

What is it to say that a nation-state-empire is, in fact, a cult, and in that, is unlike all other nations (of any size or import) who must currently negotiate amongst themselves for the world to survive and prosper? Clearly, we are not focusing on certain cult features – reverence for opaque and concrete rituals and origin stories per se – that all nations possess. What makes the US a distinctive sort of entity in this way is that every manifestation of its being is suffused with a truth that is not only a truth for everyone, but can be simply expressed and applied without limit. Had the USSR somehow survived in its post-war form, it would have served as some sort of mirror of that national form (and part of the distinctive strangeness of the Cold War resides in that contest of two cults of modernity). But even Marxism-Leninism is more willing to admit particularity and variation than Americanism – the latter organised around a few phrases, two major documents and the word 'freedom' understood in a very limited fashion.

Were we in another age, the cultishness of the United States would be of no more than academic interest to those outside of it. But we live in an era when human existence and the living nature of the planet itself can be utterly extinguished by one national power, and that is the one that most fervently believes – more than a loyal CCP Xi Jinping acolyte, a French civilisational elitist, or even an Al Qaeda wahhabist – that its national truth is not only a truth for everyone, everywhere and in all time (hence perhaps, the Mormon enthusiasm for baptising the dead), but that to be deprived of the opportunity for that way of life is to be as good as dead. The Chinese want to dominate a significant section of the world and to have a Han Chinese Communist led society recognised as superior. The Indians perhaps want the same, as far as a Hindu world ideology goes. But they all want to *live* in the world, to flourish as a nation, with their specific histories, within it. They are negotiable as to ends. What terrifies one in the American prospect is its combination of apocalyptic 'ethics' – better die than live 'unfree' – with the increasing understanding that its decline relative to other rising nations, is now either inevitable or can only be averted by switching from the commercial domination it will soon no longer be able to achieve, to a hi-tech nuclear military one, in which the end of human and planetary life is seen as an acceptable risk in the quest for domination.

There is also a nation-suicidal tinge to the perception of this decline, as expressed in the recent rise of white-skin 'Great Replacement Theory' – the idea that a sinister cabal of progressives are trying to create a multiracial, multicultural world, whose sole purpose is to hurry on the demographic decline of caucasians as punishment for their role in imperialism and colonialism. The US far right has been energised by Great Replacement Theory, even though it is a global theory, founded in European reactionary thinking. Its Americanisation can be seen in its attachment to paranoid interpretations of mundane policy proposals, such as the '15-minute city' concept – a town planning idea focused on rebuilding walkability and local shops and place into car-ravaged urban spaces. For the US proponents of 'Great Replacement', raised in ghastly post-cities of malls connected by freeways, this can be nothing other than a plan for penning in populations and introducing internal passport systems. And so on.

Where will we be if this paranoid style is taken to a pitch by a future US administration, one which combines the thuggishness of a Donald Trump with the constitutional fidelity and military world ambition that he largely eschewed? We not only need to be very interested in what happens in and to the US, we need to pressure our own governments – whose attitude to the US ranges from supine to self-sacrificial – to take a more critical approach to the shambling colossus across the Pacific.

But that said, we also need to ask a wide question about whether the term 'cult' is necessarily, wholly pejorative, and where the US sits within a wider global cult of capitalism and modernity.

Sociologists are wont to say that a religion is a cult with real estate, but it's a little more than that. Central to cults throughout history is that their beliefs are very concrete and particular, with stories playing out a closed system of oppositions and fixed meanings. One can see this in a certain type of modern cult, from Hare Krishna to Mormonism, which is pseudo-ancient, whose call is to surrender rational, abstract unbounded ways of thinking and voluntarily recommit to older ways of life. They offer a rich and compressed world of meaning that is lost in the anomie and boundarylessness of modern existence. Then there are the modern cults, which combine various forms of scientific reasoning with an underlying closed system, anchored in a charismatic figure, of which Scientology is one of the great examples.

Should a cult manage to develop beyond its initial bounds and not collapse upon itself, it can steadily spread among a wider, less organised population group, become steadily less closed in its myths and meanings, until its cultish aspects are lost to sight altogether. Christianity is the obvious example of this. The modern period – beginning with the scientific revolution of the seventeenth century – can thus be seen as the start of a long era, in which one movement after another arose that both offered the means of intellectually dismantling earlier and other cults, while having within it mechanisms that re-cultify those who adopt its ideas. Modern science began by using mathematics to demystify the workings of the natural world, so that we would understand how it worked but also be able to protect ourselves from its caprice, and make a free life for ourselves within it. In its current manifestation of Silicon Valley futurism, space worship, Meta hyperworlds, etc., it is the pursuit of a totalisation of human power that stretches beyond any purpose except the power over other humans. In the manic nihilistic obsessiveness of the Musks and Zuckerbergs, we see the anti-cult capacities of critical scientific thinking reconcretise into myths of power and transcendence.

Capitalism itself, which dictates the texture of our everyday life, may or may not be seen as a cult, depending on whether one wants to see it as a particular or general phenomenon. But one can certainly say that it uses what we go to cults for – the notion of being lifted out of the cloddish ordinariness of being human into the higher realms of desire and perfection – without any loss of the intimacies and pleasures of full human embodiment. Every advertisement for every luxury good, from holidays to furniture to food, draws on this deep need within us, offered in the form of a single object: just one more dinner mint sir, it's wafer thin. We are all the more exposed to it in a period when the consolations of neither religion, nor its secular successors such as socialism, are any longer believable.

American life is thus lived within the space of a double cult, and that might explain some of its strange parallax features: the way in which a series of atomised, frequently bad, choices can be presented as the expression of a freedom. From this perspective what looks most bizarre from the outside – for example the gleeful way in which millions of Americans resisted mask-wearing and minimal hygiene procedures during COVID, and died unnecessarily, in their tens of thousands – is necessarily logical from inside the double cult. Nothing could be more expressive of this than Ron DeSantis's push for the presidency, based on the state using its heavy hand to control the workings of school libraries, colleges, what is taught in classrooms. Rather than fight out their objections to a progressive culture – some of which have merit – at the level of ideas and debate, they are attempting to impose (recently) unprecedented state authority on everyday life. And then going to the electorate and calling it 'freedom'. And it might work.[34]

For all but the oldest and perhaps now the youngest Australians, the United States and its culture has so dominated our world that we are it, in large parts of our soul. A globalised world, a rising Asia and a more Asian population has perhaps created other spaces Australians draw from and project onto, but for most of us, it has been the US, our country's parallax otherworld, like us but also irreducibly different. Developing a critical view of the 'dangerous nation' involves, in part, an identification of that part of one's self-conception, one's hopes and personality which has been founded in and still resides there. One does not need to have ever visited the US to have been there. It would be churlish not to see much of its make-up as a gift that would not otherwise have been got. The critical and radical traditions that have grown up within it, in response to its cult of domination and its developing cult of death, have been part of the tools of our own liberation. In that we look to those undertaking that struggle and offer our solidarity and support.

# ACKNOWLEDGEMENTS

The research for this book, and some of the words, were written during coverage of the 2022 US midterms. Thanks are due to the Crikey editorial team of Jack Callil, Tom Clift and Gina Rushton; and above all to Peter Fray, for his astuteness, continuing support and forbearance. Thanks due to the many people named in these reports, and to Felicity Ruby, Dorothy Richmond, Kelsey Coots, Laura from Dauphin County, PA Democrats, and Ruy Teixeira, for their assistance. As always, many of the ideas expressed here have been developed in conversation with the editors of the 'Arena' group, and the wider circle of people who attend our 'conjuncture' discussions, and I'm grateful for their collective wisdom. Much of this book was written in the Blue Note Cafe, Richmond, one of the great old-school Melbourne cafes. Thanks to Sean, Doria and Jack for it. And to the Hardie Grant team for carving a book out of it.

# NOTES

1. Pew Research Center, 'Turnout in 2022 House midterms declined from 2018 high, final official returns show', 10 March 2023, https://www.pewresearch.org/fact-tank/2023/03/10/turnout-in-2022-house-midterms-declined-from-2018-high-final-official-returns-show/.
2. West Virginia was once a solidly Democratic state (it voted for the very liberal Mike Dukakis in 1988). It now votes Republican by more than 20 points. Manchin, a multi-millionaire from local landed family, retains the seat by being resolutely anti-green and anti-government spending. Sinema, a former Green party state politician, now represents a Democrat voting state. Despite this, she transferred to being an 'independent' after the Democrats retained Senate control in the midterms. That move lost the Democrats Senate control.
3. Trump's overall average vote in the 2016 Republican primaries was 45 per cent. However, this includes votes from late primaries, when he faced only one or two other contenders. In Iowa, the first primary, he gained 24 per cent. Averaging the first 15 primaries, gaining votes from the supporters of dropped-out candidates, he gained 33 per cent, which would appear to be a 25 per cent base, plus 8–10 per cent of new additions. Registered Republicans

comprise around 25 per cent of the US voting population. See Pew Research Center, 'Explore Party ID trends across demographics, 1992-2017', 20 March 2018, https://www.pewresearch.org/politics/2018/03/20/1-trends-in-party-affiliation-among-demographic-groups/.

4   The Tea Party's origins are multiple. In 2009, on the business channel CNBC, the presented Rick Santelli reacted to the announcement of a potential troubled mortgage-holder bailout by saying that what was needed was a new Boston tea party, a 'Chicago tea party' as he termed it, by those who had paid their mortgages. Groups around the Ron Paul movement had already started 'porculus' protests – against expanded government funding, which they saw as pork-barrelling – roasting real or fake pigs in those carparks. The idea had been suggested by shock jock commentator, the late Rush Limbaugh. After this, and Fox News, had kickstarted and branded the movement, right-wing Washington groups like Freedom Works stepped in with funding and leadership training. The Tea Party was a mix of grassroots and astroturf from the start.

5   Around 33 per cent had an undergraduate degree, 14 per cent had a higher education degree, and another 10 per cent had completed some form of higher educational study. See United States Census Bureau, 'Census Bureau Releases New Educational Attainment Data', 24 February 2022, https://www.census.gov/newsroom/press-releases/2022/educational-attainment.html.

6   Throughout his career, Trump's skill has been to make money from government concessions – The City of New York moved heaven, earth and money so he could demolish the Commodore Hotel next to Grand Central Station in the 1970s and rebuild the first of his glass edifices – and to borrow from his father, a wealthy suburban home builder. After massive near bankruptcy in the 1990s, he became little more than a 'brander' offering the Trump name to major projects for a concession, and borrowing and building overseas. See Dan Alexander, *White House, Inc.: How Donald Trump Turned the Presidency into a Business*, New York: Portfolio, 2020; and Maggie Haberman, *Confidence Man: The Making of Donald Trump and the Breaking of America*, New York: Penguin Press, 2022.

7   For more on Qanon and the Q movement see Mike Rothschild, *The Storm Is Upon Us*, New York: Melville House Publishing, 2021, which was the first book-length account of the Q movement

published. Will Sommer's more comprehensive *Trust The Plan*, New York: HarperCollins, 2023, was released after this manuscript was completed.

8  David Kirkpatrick, 'Who Is Behind QAnon? Linguistics Detectives Find Fingerprints', *The New York Times*, 19 February 2022, https://www.nytimes.com/2022/02/19/technology/qanon-messages-authors.html; for a more complex account, see Will Sommer, *Trust The Plan*, New York: HarperCollins, 2023.

9  Richard Hofstadter, *The Paranoid Style in American Politics and Other Essays*, New York: Alfred A. Knopf, 1965.

10 As the cognate form of the terms 'cult' and 'culture' indicate, cult practices are far more central to all social practices than we tend to realise. Both terms come from the literal agricultural term 'cultivation', tilling soil as metaphor. Until the nineteenth century, 'culture' was a prescriptive term, suggesting the best of the practices and texts a society had cultivated. When European imperialism brought 'intellectuals' into contact with totem and kinship-based Indigenous societies, the realisation that their entire way of life was organised around the myths prompted the notion of a 'culture'; it was first used disparagingly, then descriptively, for the process of social organisation occurring via exchange of meanings. In the twentieth century that descriptive framing was applied to modern Western societies themselves – often without considering the degree to which modern culture was organised by hidden totem figures and meaning-practices. Hence surprise when literal cults reappear to answer this deep human cultural need, and at the degree of irrationalism within public life that presents itself as reasoned. See Thomas Hylland Eriksen & Finn Sivert Nielsen eds., *A History of Anthropology*, Berkley: University of California, 2013.

11 For decades, sociologists, the most prominent being Robert Bellah, have proposed the notion of 'Americanism' – that America's fusion of civic and monotheistic themes constitutes a belief system with strong religious features. This book draws on that tradition in a very general way. For an overview, see David Gelernter, *Americanism: The Fourth Great Western Religion*, New York: Doubleday, 2007.

12 The presentation of these ideas in this book is, by necessity, vastly oversimplified and one-sided, in terms of the vast amount of scholarship and debate that have gone into concepts of American religiosity, exceptionalism and so on. For the latter, see the most

recent treatment by Australian historian Ian Tyrell, *American Exceptionalism: A New History of an Old Idea*, Chicago: University of Chicago Press, 2022.
13 The quote is from Abraham Lincoln's address to Congress, December 1862.
14 Edward Luce, interview with Barack Obama, *Financial Times*, 4 April 2009. See transcript at https://obamawhitehouse.archives.gov/the-press-office/news-conference-president-obama-4042009.
15 Remarks by the President at the United States Military Academy Commencement Ceremony, 28 May 2014. See transcript at https://obamawhitehouse.archives.gov/the-press-office/2014/05/28/remarks-president-united-states-military-academy-commencement-ceremony.
16 For the complexities of this period and process see Sam W. Haynes and Christopher Morris eds, *Manifest Destiny and Empire*, Texas: Texas A&M University Press, 2008.
17 Sean Dennis Cashman, *America In the Gilded Age*, New York: NYU Press, 1993 remains the best narrative treatment; Daniel Immerwahr, *How To Hide an Empire*, New York: MacMillan USA, 2019 is a new approach to the subsequent period.
18 Barack Obama, excerpt from speech in Berlin, available in full at 'Obama's speech in Berlin', *The New York Times*, 24 July 2008, https://www.nytimes.com/2008/07/24/us/politics/24text-obama.html.
19 Slavoj Žižek, *First As Tragedy, Then As Farce*, New York: Verso Books, 2009.
20 Josh Marcus, 'MyPillow CEO Mike Lindell says he has evidence to put 300 million in jail for election fraud', *The Independent*, 13 January 2022, https://www.independent.co.uk/news/world/americas/us-politics/mypillow-mike-lindell-2020-election-b1991885.html.
21 Edward Helmore, '"I never doubted it": Why film-maker Michael Moore forecast "blue tsunami" midterms', *The Guardian*, 14 November 2022, https://www.theguardian.com/us-news/2022/nov/14/us-midterms-film-maker-michael-moore-blue-tsunami.
22 Australian Institute of Health and Welfare (AIHW), 'Secondary education: school retention and completion', 16 September 2021, https://www.aihw.gov.au/reports/australias-welfare/secondary-education-school-retention-completion.
23 See K. Stephen Price, *Radical Reconstruction: A Brief History with Documents*, New York: Bedford Books, 2015. It is worth noting

that this interpretation is increasingly disputed, with the argument that 'radical' reconstruction is a whiteness myth, to preserve the idea of a virtuous republic.

24 The Book of Abraham, a sacred text of Mormonism, suggests a planet called 'Kolob' – closer to God than Earth – will rule over all the planets. The church has sought to minimise this 'own planet' notion, without denying it. See The Church of Jesus Christ of Latter-Day Saints, 'Becoming Like God', https://www.churchofjesuschrist.org/study/manual/gospel-topics-essays/becoming-like-god?lang=eng. Clearly, the idea is a cosmic version of the American frontier.

25 'I believe that very few men are capable of estimating the immense amount of torture and agony which this dreadful punishment, prolonged for years, inflicts upon the sufferers.' Charles Dickens, *American Notes for General Circulation*, London: Chapman & Hall, 1842.

26 The Populist movement rose in the 1880s, and was constituted as a party by the 1892 election. It had faded by the early 1900s and was opposed by those who founded the Progressive Party. It was crucial in introducing the 'primary' system of candidate selection in US political parties.

27 A 'positive freedom' interpretation of the Declaration of Independence can be made, arguing that the first of the inalienable rights to 'life, liberty and the pursuit of happiness' could be read as licensing a guarantee to the means of staying alive. But the dominant interpretation of the phrase, from the 1800s onward, has usually been that 'life' means that people should have a right to not be capriciously killed by the state, i.e. a negative freedom.

28 Remarks at the Conservative Political Action Conference Dinner, 20 March 1981, see transcript at https://www.reaganlibrary.gov/archives/speech/remarks-conservative-political-action-conference-dinner.

29 The brutal raid on the Branch Davidian church in 1993 might be seen as a last coda to the 70s cult era. This small cult grouped around preacher David Koresh was apocalyptic, heavily armed and practiced female sexual servitude to Koresh, including young teenage girls. A first raid on the compound had been lethally repelled; a second, based on heavy FBI lobbying for an assault, resulted in fires (lit by the cult, or by tear gas and other rounds

fired into their compound), and caused the death of 76 people. The alleged fear of a mass suicide event had produced a mass homicide event, a very grisly, very American outcome. Timothy McVeigh, the Oklahoma City bomber, would cite this 'Waco' siege as a motive for his actions.

30 See '1619 Project', *The New York Times Magazine*, from August 2019, https://www.nytimes.com/interactive/2019/08/14/magazine/1619-america-slavery.html.

31 A counter-interpretation of the revolution, originating with radical historian Charles Beard, argues that the event and the beliefs arising from it can only be understood in terms of the economic interests of the founders, which they turned into abstract rights. The most compelling recent such account is from Gerald Horne, *The Counter-Revolution of 1776: Slave Resistance and the Origins of the United States of America*, New York: New York University Press, 2014.

32 The US has 4.96 murders per 100,000 population per year. Australia has 0.96, the UK 1.20, Spain 0.62 See https://worldpopulationreview.com/country-rankings/murder-rate-by-country.

33 Underpinning all this, of course, is the vast power of fundamentalist Christian religion, which, as I have noted, I have spent relatively little time on. This movement can be described as a 'cult', in its transformation of a religion with a complex theology, such as Christianity, into a wilfully irrationalist cult around Biblical literalness and a 'cult of Jesus'. However, it can also be seen as something other than the key elements of cultishness I'm identifying here: their tightly bound and highly concrete and specific modalities of belief. Since the detachment of 'fundamentalism' from the Baptist and other churches in the 1920s, the movement has become an all-encompassing new religion, sharing Jesus with mainline Christianity, but constructing him, and the world, differently. In that, it is more properly treated as a religion, at least for the purposes of this short book.

34 Sinclair Lewis was said to have noted that fascism would come to America 'wrapped in the flag and carrying a cross'. The great American Marxist scholar Paul Sweezy was said to have modified it: 'when fascism comes to America, it will be called freedom'.

# Praise for *This Sucks!*

I was speechless when I finished reading this. What spirit Nick had! He went through a lot in his short life. I wish I had known him.

Edy Peterson

I've read Nick's honest, candid accounting of a portion of his life and dying process twice, as the first time through was so emotional. I'm awed by this resourceful and spiritual person, his arduous life story, and the loving "family" he created.

Jane Morgan

Fascinating. I've often passed by the trailer park where I picture Nick living wondering what life was like for people who lived there. I learned so much. I feel I know him, how he lived through things beyond my experience: his life and thought, overcoming adversity.

Judy Handke

So much to learn from Nick. What stood out for me was that he asked for what he needed. This little book will go well beyond local.

Joanne Hart

I met Nick through his.words. He made me cry and he made me laugh—so down to earth and so real. I will always love that remarkable, amazing, and caring man—the man that made himself into the man that he became. He truly made a mark on my heart. Oh, how we can learn from other's experience in life!!!!

Jo Ginther